THE STRANGE NECESSITY

By Margaret Anderson

MARGARET ANDERSON

The Strange Necessity
THE AUTOBIOGRAPHY

resolutions and reminiscence to 1969

HORIZON PRESS   NEW YORK

A Dilettante's Dedication

1961. Life was once wonderful, and so were we. This fact will be of no interest to publishers, and publishers are of no interest to me. They will reject this book about our wonderfulness, so I have written it for myself, for my wonderful friends, and (what a pleasure!) for all those who, if they should read it, would become my solemn enemies.

As a dilettante, I am free to be as light or as serious as I please. If I am seriously light, or lightly serious, what attitude could be more exhilarating, more amusing, more confusing, or more rewarding?—for all concerned. And what could be more comforting to a reading public weary of today's empty intellectualizing, merciless obscenity, and tragic young groping for something to believe in?

1968. Publisher found, to my great delight.

To Solita
with
my love, admiration,
and gratitude.

CONTENTS

Mise en scène

photograph by Victor Georg

photograph by Man Ray

a passport photograph

MARGARET ANDERSON, *the Author, in 1918, 1930, 1942.* "*I have no imagination, I can write only of the people, places and things I have known and loved—or not loved. And since all my characters are real people, I shall name them in advance: . . .*"

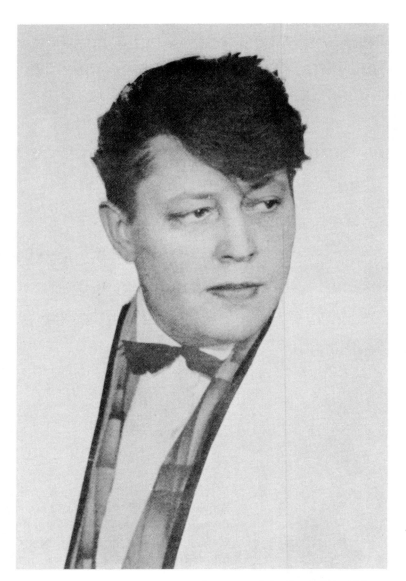

photograph by Berenice Abbott

"...JANE HEAP, co-editor of the 'Little Review', and later founder of a Gurdjieff group in London ..."

"...GEORGETTE LEBLANC, singer, actress, writer. Author of 'Souvenirs, Vol. I: My Life with Maeterlinck'. Vol. II: 'La Machine à Courage'..."

"... DOROTHY CARUSO, wife of the tenor. Author of 'Enrico Caruso — His Life and Death'. And 'A Personal History'..."

photograph by Berenice Abbott

"... SOLITA SOLANO, author of a beautiful book of poetry with the beautiful title, 'Statue in a Field'..."

photograph by Berenice Abbott

"...*JANET FLANNER*, '*Genet*' *of* '*The New Yorker*',
author of '*Men and Monuments*', '*Paris Journal, 1944-
1964*', *etc.* . . ."

"...'MONIQUE', 'a character met only in
books with coloured illustrations'..."

"...GEORGE I. GURDJIEFF, author of 'All and Everything', and gradually becoming known as the major prophet of our time ..."

"...ALFRED A. ORAGE, one-time editor of the English 'New Age', and known to many in New York as the precursor and interpreter of Gurdjieff in the twenties and thirties."

Five Foreword

I have never been conscious of anything except of being identified with a fantasy—that I came from nowhere, out of nothing, into nothing, and that I made up a life that was different from others. I lived that life just as I wanted to, though most of the time there was no reason to believe that it could be done.

The curious thing is that all this is true. I felt that I had been born on a Christmas Eve, when I sat before a Christmas tree and heard "Silent Night" for the first time and wanted to cry; and then found a tiny white kitten with a large pink bow around its neck sleeping in my doll's cradle. Everything has gone on from this, just like this, and it was all so unlike what I saw happening around me—happier, more fantastic, more enviable, greater in love and friendship—that it is still hard to believe; because I have never seen, or heard of, or read about, anyone living a life just like mine. I am too superstitious to boast about it, but too egoistic not to prize it, and I should like to find an appropriate title for such a manic life story—something like "Remembrance of Things Present"—that is, my Past; or "The Strange Necessity."

1. The "Little Review" Credo

In 1914, having nothing to offer to the world of Art except appreciation, I had the temerity to start a magazine of the arts —the *Little Review*. I was very young, and Arthur Davidson Ficke asked me, "So you're launching a magazine of new prose! Are you sure you know all there is to know about great classic prose?" "Of course not," I said, "I only know that there's something new and exciting in the air, and that I'm going to like it. I want to know the people who are making it, I want to hear their conversation. I want to publish them."

That's all there was to it—my start from nothingness to what, through others, became something.

The *Little Review* began in August 1914, and for a year or more contained the best "new" things I could find. Then, at a moment when I was searching for more brilliant material, I met Jane Heap. She impressed me as someone who knew about everything that matters in the world of great ideas—the kind of thing that other magazines didn't offer. Her talk was a natural art, and her mind (in my opinion) so outran others that I wanted it, above all else, for the magazine.

Thus our golden age began. "With beauty aghast"—this was our state. How we urged it upon others, how we talked, how we thought, how we wrote! How grateful our audience was! We, the spellbound, lived a celebration.

Even today, in an age when beauty mustn't be mentioned, I believe that a longing for such celebration still exists, somewhere. Surely, somehow, somewhere, it can still be evoked for the undernourished of today's dismal world.

I love yesterday, I deplore today, and I am hopeful of tomorrow because it can't be so bad as today.

I am tired of "new writing" and of "powerful new novelists."
I am tired of today's new people; I'm tired of their lives, of their
tastes, their reading, their language, their singing, their seda-
tives and their psychiatrists, their houses, their furniture, and
their faces.

What am I most tired of? Today's arid poets.

What do I most loathe? Today's rancid sex books.

All this being so, I have written about what I most love. And
I love more things than I loathe.

All the ideas I loved are less understood today than they
were when I was young . . . for instance, our authentic defense
of the art-for-art's-sake theory, which can be formulated in words
Jane found, long ago, for our *Little Review* credo:

TO EXPRESS THE EMOTIONS OF LIFE IS TO LIVE.
TO EXPRESS THE LIFE OF EMOTIONS IS TO MAKE ART.

2. MY ATOMIC AGE

Before continuing my story I must further describe my present mise en scène and my characters, that is—my friends.

Since this is the atomic age, it is easy for me to imagine that bombs have devastated the country in which I have lived for over forty years. All the places that were my homes in France have been demolished or have disappeared. Two have been destroyed, two desecrated, two modernized, one transformed, and two have fallen into decay.

The beautiful Pavillon des Muses, in Neuilly, where we lived as "family" guests, has been razed to make room for a high apartment building. Sometimes called the Palais des Muses, and supposed to have been a pied-à-terre of Louis XIV, it was one of the gems of France and the home of Robert de Montesquieu in Proustian days.

The exquisite house in Paris, 18 rue Vaneau, with its garden of high, dark trees—which we rented when we were supposed to be rich—has been torn down and replaced by a towering building of flats. It was here that Ezra Pound first met George Antheil and urged him to write "Abstraction and Time in Music," which we printed in the *Little Review*—an article with which I still disagree. It was here that Brancusi, Marcel Duchamp, Picabia, and Fernand Léger played hide-and-seek with us in the great salons.

The magnificent Château de Tancarville in Normandie—where we lived in the splendour of a tower once supposed to have housed Marie Stuart—still stands, but the Germans ploughed up the lawns, cut down many of the ancient trees, and no one lives there today but a gardien-concierge. In summer unfortunate children (fortunate to vacation here) sleep in the beautiful bedrooms, and use the salons as their untidy playrooms.

The Château de Rocheville, in St.-Germain-en-Laye—where my last nightingale sang—survives externally, but the interior has been done over into apartments.

The haunting Château de la Muette, our Louis XV's hunting-lodge deep in the forest of St. Germain, has been taken over as a radio station. Stripped of all its past, what remains of "la folie de Louis XV"? It has become a glaring white villa, its windows reduced from grandeur to suburban dimensions, its decorative curved shutters removed. Once the scene of royal festivities, where Marie Antoinette's fête-de-fiançailles was celebrated, it has now become a monument of the Cinquième République. Only the chestnut trees still stand, unchanged, and the old stone well beneath them. In autumn their leaves still fall in spirals of gold, "returning gently to the earth."

The desecration of our lighthouse in Tancarville—a short walk through a forest to the château—is even more painful. It is now inhabited by people of that pretentious class just above the peasantry. They have torn out its fireplaces, abolished its sailors' alcoves, built a grey cement veranda across its front, and furnished it with modern sets from the Bon Marché. Unwarned, Monique and I revisited it. The sight so unnerved us that she fell and broke her arm.

The famous Abbaye de St. Wandrille, where Georgette and Maeterlinck lived for so many years, has been given back to the Benedictines.

The lovely Château du Prieuré, in Fontainebleau-Avon, where Madame de Maintenon once lived and where Gurdjieff had his Institute for the Harmonious Development of Man, is now also Church property.

And our poignant Paris flat, at 17 rue Casimir Périer, where we lived when we were dedicating our lives to Gurdjieff, has fallen into such decay that I try to turn my eyes away when I pass by. For years, on the anniversary of Georgette's death, we placed a red rose beside our door on the fourth floor. We didn't know who the new tenants were, or whether they wondered about the roses.

Of all the beauty and splendour I have known in France, only one place remains as it was—the Chalet Rose in Le Cannet, on a hill two miles above Cannes. It is probably the smallest house in which three people ever lived (barring Russian houses), and it was our war refuge when we had no other place to go. It has two rooms and a kitchen, running water (cold), no bath.

After living in all the palaces, Georgette and Monique and I lived together during the war in the Chalet Rose. Georgette died there in 1941. Monique, the perfect companion, lived on with me there until she died in 1961, when she was ninety-two.

3. ALL MY LOVELY COMPANIONS

As after a final holocaust, nearly everyone who made life wonderful for me has died. All my lovely companions—nearly all—are faded and gone.

They are the characters in this story and, living or dead, they are all people of special quality. All of them but one are writers of books, and all of them have appeared in books. There are two others who don't appear: one, my favourite enemy; the other, my favourite friend.

For some of the descriptions I shall steal from another friend, a painter of souvenir-portraits—Elspeth Champcommunal, whose emotional intelligence has endowed her with the powers of observation necessary for the art of evocation:

GEORGETTE LEBLANC. "Of all my memories of her—her green eyes flashing, lengthened or narrowed or wide open and smiling and seeming to reflect water—I remember best a sort of enchantment round her when once, in Giverny, she read us passages from the book she was then writing. She was wearing a kind of hat and over it some sort of soft cream chiffon which was also swathed round her neck (this was in the garden, I must tell you). She had on enormous horn spectacles and I think no make-up, and I cannot tell you how exquisitely ethereal her face looked as she read, really as one imagines a spirit to be; and her voice and the flow of her divine French were utterly unforgettable."—*Elspeth Champcommunal*

JANE HEAP. "That Jane exists in the way she does fills people with strength and new realizations in those parts of their beings which sometimes shrivel emotionally. She is always staunchly herself, and her humour, always flickering, delights one. Though she is overwhelmed with work, and fatigue and illness, she endures it all with the utmost fortitude. When one is under great

23

strain, for which no words can be found, she always finds the right way to prove that she has understood through all one's incoherence. She becomes a kind of benign wizard, warm and with a mysterious kindness and affection. She is like a 'home' in herself, full of a loving security which banishes tensions, so that one becomes, momentarily, a new being."—*Elspeth Champcommunal*

DOROTHY CARUSO. "I have thought of Dorothy's presence as I knew it, the calm and beauty and gaiety of those huge blue eyes, the steady warmth and kindness of her existence. I remember so well her voice and laugh and sudden little sallies that were never malicious, her bearing and patience and courage and a curious feeling of stability and peace she gave, even to people who were not her intimate friends, like myself; and I also have a feeling of someone 'let in' close to her, when I think of our marvelous days in Sudbury and other moments in London and Giverny. Someone you could never possibly forget."—*Elspeth Champcommunal*

SOLITA SOLANO. I have no portrait of her—which doesn't matter, since she can speak so well for herself. Some of her formulations:

"One must have standards. They are not easily come by.

"Beauty should be evoked, not bluntly stated from subconscious processes.

"A thought should be a conclusion, engendered by an antithesis, or a homogeneity. 'Thinking out aloud' does not produce quality of thought.

"Gurdjieff once said, 'I know you "think" at home, but here (at my table) must be quintessence.' So should a book be also—quintessence, traces of the crucible; if not 'Art,' at least *métier*. I stopped writing because I had only *métier* for public approval."

JANET FLANNER. Although Janet's prose is famous, her special genius as translator is less known. Therefore I quote her rendering of St. John Perse's tribute to President Kennedy which appeared in *Le Monde*, in Paris:

Il combattit à l'arme franche, et sa rencontre avec la mort fut à visage découvert . . . Il avait ce regard clair et droit des jeunes chefs formés à l'amitié humaine.

(He fought always with his weapons unhidden, and in his meeting with death his face was uncovered . . . He had the clear, direct gaze of those young chiefs formed for friendship with mankind.)

For some reason, one isn't particularly moved by the French "formed for human friendship." But "formed for friendship with mankind" is a trouvaille that stops the breath for a moment.

"MONIQUE." "Monique is a fairy-tale nurse, a character met only in books with coloured illustrations, a nature without angles, a being whose words and steps make no sound and who always offers to agree with me."—*Georgette Leblanc*

"Monique is a complete person. She makes things happen in rooms simply by being in them; this she has done for years and years. It is an act of sensitivity that by use has become something like creation. She possesses a remarkable repose that is neither conscious nor unconscious, though in the beginning it might have been either. She has the ease of a child who speaks or keeps silent as it chooses, and in all my life I've never met anyone with greater dignity. She is like a bird and a cat, unimpressed by her surroundings. She contains a world, but invites few people nowadays to share it—or enter it—so people rarely realize that it exists. She neither keeps young, nor grows old, but has a fixed quantity like a star in time."—*Dorothy Caruso*

A. R. ORAGE. A letter from John Cowper Powys,* after Orage had talked with him and his wife about Gurdjieff:
    "Your visit to us was the greatest event of our winter! . . . We came to the conclusion that whatever ambiguousness there may be in the nature of your mythology, there must be something profoundly right in your attitude towards it. There's something so 'fixed-up,' so unctuous and conceited about these Indian swamies and esoteric teachers . . . something that is unilluminating and does not vibrate to the shocks of real life, something that seems to face life through wads of cotton wool.
    "We go on puzzling ourselves as to exactly what it is that makes your philosophy so different from this; what it is that

---

* Quoted by Stanley Nott from *On Love, with Some Aphorisms and Other Essays* by A. R. Orage (London: The Janus Press).

makes it so fresh and natural and faltering and troubled, as all genuine attitudes to life ought to be . . . We got the impression of actually and really—(don't be angry now!)—having entertained a real Saint that day . . . As if you had been a person in armour but who was secretly bleeding from wounds invisible. You didn't convert us one inch . . . to your particular gods or ritual or doctrines or master. But you compelled us and still compel us to accept yourself in your present mood as possessed of some extraordinary psychic secret—one great portion of which is a kind of transcendental humility, or whatever it may be.

"I think we both snatched at some drop of this virtue or aura or emanation and have used it ever since as a test of spiritual values. It is extraordinary. You alone of all men of genius I have ever met seem totally to have conquered pride . . . You certainly made us think a lot, and as for anything 'fantastic' about it all—we are entirely with you there. In the 'fantastic' lies the essence of things."—*John Cowper Powys*

A portrait of GURDJIEFF? I can't find one that will do, except in his own words. They should efface the disastrous impressions given out by some of the unsure and complicated Gurdjieff followers who had no simplicity of their own with which to meet and measure his:

"The fact of the matter is that in occult literature much has been said that is superfluous and untrue. You had better forget all this. All your researches in this region were a good exercise for your mind; therein lies their great value, but only there. They have not given you knowledge. Judge everything from the point of view of your common sense; become the possessor of your own sound ideas and don't accept anything on faith; and when you, your own self, by way of sound reasoning and argument, come to an unshaken persuasion, to a full understanding of something, then you will have achieved a certain degree of initiation. Think it over more deeply . . . For instance, remember this conversation; *think.* In essence I have told you nothing new . . . The only thing I did was to bring your knowledge into order. I systematized it, but you had it before you saw me. You owed it to the efforts already made by you in this field.

26

In a year's time we may say the same things, but you will have *worked,* your understanding will have changed—you will be more initiated. It is impossible to give a man anything that could become his inalienable property without work on his part. Such initiation cannot be. There is only 'self-initiation.' The teacher can show and direct, but not 'initiate.' And before speaking, he must know and see how much such a man can understand. *Understanding* comes only with work."—*Gurdjieff*

A portrait of the AUTHOR? A comment of Jane Heap's—in two words—will serve:

Someone asked her, "What is Margaret's book about?"
Jane, with a loud laugh, "Herself—fiction!"

4. FICTION?

My fiction has a solid basis of fact—the fact being that I am in the shameful position of a person to whom life has been too kind. I seem to have been spared the ugly, the lonely, and the too difficult. I have never had to work for a living. I have worked, but always at something that has pleased or interested me. I have sometimes gone hungry—for Art, or because of war—but never for too long. I have always been well, except for minor mishaps caused by pleasure, greed, or ignorance. I have never had an operation, and I had my first physical check-up at seventy-two. I have never taken vitamin pills. I have never taken a tranquilizer, or an aspirin tablet, or a sleeping pill—I have my own methods for capturing sleep. I have been given a nature that loves music with a blinding, dizzying exaltation. I have been endowed with the mysterious energy necessary for the creation of an extra life—I sometimes spend a speechless, sleepless night over a great poem, a page of great prose, or a disque of great music which I play over and over until dawn. I have lost the friends I most deeply loved, but the love endures and shields me from loneliness. I feel so young that, though I think of death, I don't think of age. I am an astonished stranger to the squalid sex moeurs of today's fiction and autobiography. I have never been related to government or politics, to that blind, stupid, heavy thing known as "law" . . . or to any other external activity. I have never felt that I could help the world in any way except when, at twenty-five, I thought I was an artist and an anarchist and founded the *Little Review;* I have never joined a group of any kind except, much later, when I came to know Gurdjieff's teaching and felt myself lost in outer space. I have always fought for ideas—until I learned that it isn't ideas but grief, struggle,

and flashes of vision which enlighten. I have always been a
propagandist for my own theories of what is, and what is not Art,
and I haven't been able to give up this dictatorship. I have never
been able to make money, but, as if by divine dispensation, I have
been provided with enough to live on and to help a few friends
in a few ways. I happen to be living—at first by accident, later
by design—in a place that has been called an earthly paradise,
and my present occupations are Life, Liberty, and the pursuit of
Loveliness. (By "life" I now mean an effort to understand what
appears at first to be beyond understanding, but which, by stages,
can become known.)

It is now my immense pleasure and privilege to live outside the
grave new world of today, far from the vehemence of cities and
the violence of events.

It's not that I object to the way others want to live. It's not
that I would try to dissuade anyone from flying to the moon if he
feels like it. But I have never flown from one city to another. I've
never been in a plane, and I shall never get into one. I wouldn't
feel natural in the sky.

There are lots of other things I've never done. For one, I've
never found a four-leaf clover—some things don't come naturally
to me. The least natural of all would be to risk burning to death
in an airplane. I also try to escape being drowned, or trapped
under a wrecked train. I avoid ships and trains when I can,
I've remained firmly fixed in the era of the automobile; there
my life is in my own expert hands, and head—and reflexes. I
never sail on a ship or ride on a train today without wishing
that I were the captain or the engineer—instead of those two
unknown characters who are assuming the responsibility of my
existence. I want, in all situations, to be at the controls. I enjoy
safety, though for years I never gave it a thought. Now it is a
passion. Not long ago I saved the lives of a dozen people in a bus
left carelessly standing on a hill, by leaping into the driver's

empty seat and pulling the brakes. The irresponsible driver came running after us. "Mon dieu, madame, merci!! Quelle présence d'esprit!"

In any case I certainly have enough présence d'esprit to stay on the ground instead of flying through heaven. Cosmic space is my idea of the ultimate anti-natural.

I haven't the slightest desire to roam around the sun, I have no wish to approach the mysterious moon. "As above, so below" . . . this is a statement that interests me. It suggests great questions. For instance: "There is a sun in man. What is it?" Or this: "The moon . . . Every outer manifestation has its psychological replica. Some part of our psychology bears the same relation to us that the moon bears to our psychic life. Therefore, what is the moon in man?" If these questions can be answered, why not here on our own planet?—after we have learned something about the *probable* cosmic rotation of our present into our future universe. I see no reason to believe that the answers will be found on Moon, Mars, or Venus rather than on Earth.

So I shall continue to love life on the earth and all its ancient rituals.

I love shadowed rooms and wood fires, tall libraries full of subtle and leisurely books, accomplished conversations that flow for hours. I love *essential* people; their minds, their faculties, their bearing, awe me. I also love people who have grace and flair, lightness of touch, and touching awarenesses—people who are used to being human beings; I love their predicament in the modern world—it makes for the best conversation. I love people who love their isolation from the outside world—why shouldn't they be allowed to cultivate their inner worlds? I love ivory towers—the right kind for the right people. Towers are sanity for those who are at home in them—happy, absorbed, and inspired; those who feel nervous, uneasy, doubtful, guilty, bored, lonely, empty, or unhappy in towers can easily come

down to earth again. I am a "happy" person, therefore a tower
for me is a tower of strength.

"You're living in a forgotten world," people tell me.

True, true, a world too good to be true. But *forgotten?* Can
I forget the criteria we lived by? They existed outside le monde
matière, they belonged to the world which great art projects.
Our poets weren't sterile, our novelists had important human
reasons for telling their stories. They wrote about the inside of
life rather than the outside (which gives an impression of "no-
body home"). With us, nothing was called "great" simply because it was written intellectually. Our intellectuals didn't make
status symbols of calculated ambiguity, complicated vacuity,
clinical brutality, or concentrated ugliness; and the simple honest public—which, when left to its own judgments, usually knows
by instinct what's what—isn't afraid to call the "too beautiful"
Bach aria great music. Ah, if I could launch a *Little Review*
today! *We* knew that intellectuals aren't sure arbiters; we knew
that certain subject-matters lie forever outside the province of
Art; we knew that Art is produced from, and confers, an uncommon, irrefutable experience, and we could talk all night about
what that experience was. The mystery of it gave us an additional formula for our credo:

*INTELLECTUALS DO NOT HAVE
AESTHETIC EXPERIENCES.*

Aesthetic experience is as enduring as experience in a par-
allel, visible world. How can anyone forget:

Shadows on stone walls, lilacs in the doorway, the blue evenings of autumn, "the falling snow, the hour before the dawn,"
hearth fires and sleeping kittens, tall forests in mist, violets in
deep woods, summer lanes, rain in the night, water-lily lakes,
the courtyards of country inns, the presence of trees, shadows
on the grass, sails on silent water, music at midnight, poems of

sorrow, birds and church bells, castle towers, books of old tales, childhood's candy, Christmas stars, candlelight and roses, pianos and fountains, the sadness of moonlight, songs of love . . .

And love itself—love of life, love of nature, love of art, love of beauty, love of truth, love of beauty, love of mind, love of beauty, love of beauty!!, love of love, love of self (oh dear!), love of others, love of one other . . .

Unforgettable, unforgotten . . .

Life now seems to pass around me, not through me. It is as if I have already lived everything I have a need to live. But I have lived such a celebration . . . what Montaigne called "an absolute perfection, resembling divinity—to know how to enjoy one's own being."

5. REALITIES

I have known three realities.

The first was defined, over 2000 years ago, by Mang-tse, as "the mere business of living, the dull grinding attribution of everyday which has at last unfitted the human race for life." This non-life has always been my greatest enemy, and I have fought it successfully for over sixty years.

The second reality is my own. I was apparently born with it, and it has served me well. Or should I say—ill?

The third reality—the important one—should be written with a capital R, and I have only glimpsed it. I have tried to impose it upon my personal reality and have made some progress. But my own has remained so strong, so vivifying, so crippling (?), so dazzling, that I want to write about it, about what I have chiefly celebrated: the life of emotions superimposed upon the emotions of life.

PART ONE

THE LIFE OF ART

This phrase, I believe, is Rebecca West's, and I use it to leap into the subject-matter I love: the strange necessity of the artist, the strange need of the appreciator. I am the appreciator per se.

I don't want to talk about the arts. My interest is in *Art as a state* . . . that strange ultimate state of great creation—"the white-hot coal . . . as steady and sustained as a flame in a windless place."

This state is my subject, and this alone. I have spent my life thinking about it, searching for it in every book I read, in all the music I listen to, in every gallery I visit. When you come upon it you have a moment of *the great reward,* like my experience of walking into Brancusi's studio years ago in Paris, and suddenly stopping before his Golden Bird (*Bird in Space*). I lost my breath. I knew I had been projected into the great state of Art.

(If I had an art gallery I would give the *Bird in Space* a small room to itself, in the center of which it would soar, with Victory-of-Samothrace impulsion, against a background of faint blue sky. I wonder why no one has ever thought of doing this.)

Of course there are admirable works of art that never attain the fiery state. There are masterpieces of prose, poetry, music, painting, sculpture, which never, or rarely, burn at white heat. In all the books of great literature it is possible to read ten, twenty pages at a time without once coming upon a phrase like the flame in a windless space. When you do, you are left breathless.

I was so breathless in *Little Review* days that people told me the gesture I made most often (unconscious on my part) was to place my left hand, fingers outspread, against my heart. I must have felt that it had stopped beating and needed my protection. When I was made conscious of the gesture I stopped making it. But Alice Toklas told me not long ago that when we first met in 1923, this gesture had convinced her and Gertrude Stein that I was a lightweight, a scatterbrain, an "ecstatic." I'm glad that she changed her mind later. But Gertrude never did. She and I got off to a bad start. The first thing she said to me was that I had no right to publish young writers in the *Little Review* without paying them. I was extremely irritated. "It's not a question of right," I said, "but of duty. No one else will publish them." This irritated *her,* and we went from bad to worse. Alice and I became great friends, but I could never agree with her estimation of Gertrude's "genius." If one were ever free to say exactly what one thinks, I would have said to her: "I dislike immensely Gertrude's type of egoism; her awesome self-enamouration shows itself either as a comfortable, chuckling kind (which isn't too unsympathetic), or as a grotesque, arrogant kind as when she announced on meeting a

Frenchwoman for the first time, 'I am a genius, one of the greatest in the world today'—which seemed to me slightly insane.
The Frenchwoman said, 'She frightened me.'" I was also put off
by an atmosphere of commercialism that I felt emanating around
Gertrude like an aura. It made me uncomfortable, as if I were
in a place where I didn't belong. I've held my reaction to her
in check for so long, as I've listened to all the eulogies, that it's
a relief to say what I really thought about her. The "strange
necessity" emits a different emanation.

People are always arguing about the laws of aesthetics. Janet Flanner begins her interesting *Men and Monuments* with the statement (like Tolstoy's) that there are no permanent criteria for judging what is, and what is not, Art.

Dear Janet, and Tolstoy, how wrong you are! This is the most easily deflated theory in the world. That artists disagree among themselves about standards, that styles change, that connoisseurs denounce and devalue what they once esteemed—all this has no more bearing on the aesthetic situation than the fact that statesmen are at first extolled and then deposed. To be quite simple, Millet's *Angelus* will always be a work of art: the background, the foreground, and the figures in the landscape . . . a moving evocation of universe, earth, and man's aspirations—the peasants have stopped work and bowed their heads in prayer. You can't look at it without being lifted out of your everyday mood (unless you're not a touchstone for what is moving). It is Art—it falls within the Nine Eternal Moods.

These moods reflect the permanent life of the affirmed emotions of mankind. The *form* in which they are cast (scarcely definable) determines whether the expressed emotions will endure or fade. Their potential permanence is the most enthralling of considerations: in the greatest Art, in which both the subject-matter and the treatment must be great; or in lesser Art, in which a dish of apples and lemons must be expressed "greatly," that is, by exagération à propos.

"But," someone always objects, "what *is* appropriate exaggeration and what isn't? And *who* knows what is and what isn't? You're involved again in the old dispute about permanent criteria."

"No, no," I say. Here is a distinguishing definition of Art that I like more than others:

> Un monde vous frappe dans la poitrine et abolit tout ce qui n'est pas lui.—*Georgette Leblanc.*
> (A world strikes you in the heart and leaves you unconscious of everything except it.)

"This happens in whose heart?"

"For one, in mine."

"But why is your heart more sensitive than others?"

"I don't know why, but it often is."

"You are insufferable."

"Perhaps. But I always know when to lose my breath, and when to weep."

"Don't all people?"

"Not if you listen to what they say."

"Whom does your vanity consider a judge of breathlessness or tears?"

"Anyone who loses his breath or weeps at the right moments."

"Who knows what are the right moments?"

"Anyone who is a touchstone."

"But *who* are touchstones?"

"Those who are born touchstones. Who are artists? Those who are born artists."

No one, to me, has defined the touchstone's position more clearly than Orage, in his *Readers and Writers,* in an essay on "Right Criticism":

> It may be said that if we dismiss personal preference as a criterion of art judgment, there is either nothing left or only some "scientific" standard which has no relevance to aesthetics. It is the common plea of the idiosyncrats that, inconclusive as their opinions must be, and anything but universally valid, no other method within the world of art is possible. I dissent. A "final" judgment is as possible of a work of art as of any other manifesta-

tion of the spirit of man; there is nothing in the nature of things to prevent men arriving at a universally valid (that is, universally accepted) judgment, of a picture, a sonata, a statue, or a building any more than there is to prevent a legal judge from arriving at a right judgment concerning any other human act; and, what is more, such judgments of art are not only made daily, but in the end they actually prevail and constitute in their totality the tradition of art. The test is not scientific, but as little is it merely personal. Its essential character is simply that it is right; right however arrived at, and right whoever arrives at it. That the judge in question may or may not have "studied" the history of the art-work he is judging is a matter of indifference. Neither his learning nor his natural ignorance is of any importance. . . All that matters is that his judgment, when delivered, should be "right." But who is to settle this? it may be asked. Who is to confirm a right judgment or to dispute a wrong one? The answer is contained in the true interpretation of the misunderstood saying, *De gustibus non est disputandum.* The proof of right is that there is no real dispute about its judgment; its finality is evidenced by the cessation of debate. The truth may be simply stated: a judge—that is to say, a true judge—is he with whom everybody is compelled to agree, not because he says it, but because it is so.

TOUCHSTONES

A letter from Solita: "Instead of rebelling about what is happening in today's world, why don't you write about what happens in *your* world? You have in your head (and heart) a treasure-trove of rare trivia which under your treatment could become major incidents of life. Get out your miner's outfit and dig for gold."

Nothing could give me greater pleasure. My lovely, incessant trivia . . . a serious dilettante's attitude toward such subjects as beauty, truth, love, and art.

"You think you're always right about everything," says an enemy.

"I don't. I think I'm always right for *myself*. My standards are the discredited ones of 'I like' or 'I don't like.' For me, then, to prove what my 'self' is worth."

As a touchstone, I divide my responses to Art into four categories. The first produces loss of breath; the second, tears; the third, musical reward; the fourth, mental reward. Such rewards are usually contained in a word, a phrase, a paragraph, and the French have the best name for them—les trouvailles; not maxims, aphorisms, or epigrams, but a new or striking or moving way of combining simple words for vitality of emotion.

Critics often disagree with me about trouvailles. When Ezra Pound was foreign editor of the *Little Review* he produced an admirable French number, devoted to the new French poets. But he didn't mention Apollinaire, or quote that poet's most perfect poem—the five lines that compose "L'Adieu." When Oscar Williams published an anthology of modern poets he included just two of Joyce's. . . . "I Hear an Army"? "Ecce Puer"? Not

43

at all. He chose "The Holy Office" and "The Ballad of Persse O'Reilly"!!

Examples of my four categories, which I shall choose at random from books that have come to me recently, or from memories of unforgettable passages, phrases, nouns, verbs, adjectives that have persisted in my emotions for years.

First Category—Loss of Breath

One night last winter, at midnight, I opened a book—a collection, *The Best Short Stories of Edith Wharton,* edited by Wayne Andrews. Instead of reading the first story first, I began with one I had never read before, "Bunner Sisters" . . . a simple story of two sisters, little spinster shopkeepers, who have lived alone together for years. One day the younger, Evelina, marries and goes away. After the marriage, these two paragraphs:

> Eliza Ann was duly grateful for the neighbors' kindness, but the "talking over" on which they had evidently counted was Dead Sea fruit on her lips; and just beyond the familiar warmth of their presences she saw the form of Solitude at her door.
> Eliza Ann was but a small person to harbor so great a guest, and a trembling sense of insufficiency possessed her. She had no high musings to offer to the new companion of her hearth. Every one of her thoughts had hitherto turned to Evelina and shaped itself in homely easy words; of the mighty speech of silence she knew not the earliest syllable.

As I read "the mighty speech of silence" I lost my breath. Here was the miracle, and I participated in it as Edith Wharton must have presided over its creation. I sat on until two o'clock in the morning, absolutely still—I remember being aware of how still I was, and how surprised when I looked at my clock . . . I had been repeating over and over, in awed appreciation, those five words—the incomparable adjective "mighty" and the perfect

44

noun "speech." Had she said "the mighty language of silence" the magic would have been less. This sentence became the event of my winter.

Why did it so move me? Because it represents the distinction I've been talking about—the difference between expressing the *emotions of life* and the *life of emotions.* The heroine of the story is living one of the great emotions of life; the author of the story needn't have commented, she could simply have continued the narrative. But she was possessed by that strange necessity which led her to the language of FORM— "moulded into the purpose of the impulse that engendered it."

Another example, so simple that you can't explain why your breath is stopped for a second. (Marcel Proust, *Remembrance of Things Past*):

Albertine was dead. Ah! Never again would I enter a forest. . .

Another: Isak Dinesen's short story, "The Dreaming Child," in *Winter Tales.* The two exceptional adjectives, followed by the surprising noun, "unity":

. . . Jan gave himself up to, and was absorbed by, the boundless, final unity of dreams.

Also Dinesen, in *Out of Africa:*

. . . a herd of elephants travelling through dense Native forest . . . pacing along as if they had an appointment at the end of the world.

Idea of a movie script, by James Agee (*Letters to Father Flye*): All thirty-six elephants die in a fire.

Their huge souls, light as clouds, settle like doves in the great secret cemetery back in Africa.

Leonard Bernstein:

The opening of the third act of *La Bohème* in a series of cold, empty fifths, raining like snowflakes over the stage.

. . . as if it had been painted by a bird.—*Jean Cocteau*
. . . the perfect facts of the open air.—*Walt Whitman*
. . . amid the romance of great trees.—*George Moore*
. . . as sleepless always as fire.—*Charles Algernon Swinburne*
. . . the verb, angel of movement.—*Charles Baudelaire*
. . . the circles of intelligence in the heavens.—*Plato*
. . . the distant approach of things mighty and magnificent.—*William Blake*
. . . Harmony itself is a thing of thought.—*Richard Wagner*
. . . words which startle by their delicate resemblance to thoughts.—*Arthur Symons*
. . . Into a land of mirrors without time or space.—*W. H. Auden*
And the sheen of their spears
Was as foam on the sea.—*Homer*
Study me, then, you who shall lovers be,
For I am a very dead thing.—*Christopher Marlowe*

Joyce's *Portrait of the Artist as a Young Man.* The last sentence:

He watched their flight, bird after bird; a dark flash, a swerve, a flutter of wings . . . Their cry was shrill and clear and fine and falling like threads of silken light unwound from whirling spools.

Joyce's *Dubliners:*

It had begun to snow again . . . It was falling on every part of the dark central plain . . . It was falling, too, upon the lonely churchyard on the hill . . . His soul swooned slowly as he heard the snow falling faintly through the universe and faintly falling, like the descent of their last end, upon the living and the dead.

My Second Category—Tears

This category is more difficult to define. I think of Poe's "Annabel Lee" . . . If you try to read it aloud you lose your voice. In my lifetime I've known only one person who has been insensitive to this poem—she said it made her feel nothing at all.

Christina Rossetti's "Uphill" produces a deep quality of tears, especially if you have known Gurdjieff. It is as if she had learned what he had to teach, and learned that it can be lived. Since no one reads it today, I quote it in full:

Does the road wind uphill all the way?
> Yes, to the very end.
Will the day's journey take the whole long day?
> From morn to night, my friend.

But is there for the night a resting-place?
> A roof for when the slow, dark hours begin.
May not the darkness hide it from my face?
> You cannot miss that inn.

Shall I meet other wayfarers at night?
> Those who have gone before.
Then must I knock, or call when just in sight?
> They will not keep you waiting at that door.

Shall I find comfort, travel-sore and weak?
> Of labour you shall find the sum.
Will there be beds for me and all who seek?
> Yes, beds for all who come.

Joyce's "Ecce Puer" is so moving that you can't even think of it without weeping. The last two lines overwhelm you.

Of the dark past
A child is born;
With joy and grief
My heart is torn.

Calm in his cradle
The living lies.
May love and mercy
Unclose his eyes.

Young life is breathed
On the glass;
The world that was not
Comes to pass.

A child is sleeping,
An old man gone.
O, father forsaken,
Forgive your son!

I always remember a poem by Richard Dixon (1855–1910), written after the death of his wife—just four lines:

She comes not: in the summer night
The trembling river runneth bright.
O look again, fond heart of love,
On darkling earth, on heaven above.

What are the most touching lines Proust ever wrote: after the death of his grandmother—perhaps the saddest paragraph in all literature?

Et je ne demandais rien de plus à Dieu, s'il existe un paradis . . . qu'il me laissât rester avec elle toute l'éternité, qui ne serait pas trop longue pour nous deux.

(And I would not ask more of God, if there is a paradise, than that he would allow me to remain with her for all eternity, which would not be too long for either of us.)

There is Victor Hugo's "En Souvenir d'Elle," and I think of Donne, Marlowe, Keats, Verlaine, Emily Brontë, and all the others . . .

Yes, I know that the mission of Art is "to dry all tears," so perhaps I should call this category *Poignancy*. Some very sad poems don't make you weep but hold you silent and startled by their genius, like James Wright's "The Avenger," surely the most beautiful poem of today's world, and which I believe has received no prize:

> She—the woman whom I loved
> Longer than her beauty lasted,
> Loved as long as starlight moved
> Carefully around the earth—
> Lies behind me, old in death,
> All her quiet patience wasted.
>
> Now I walk beneath the night,
> Having watched her die all day.
> Rain veils soft the bedroom light
> Where I held her in my arms.
> What blind movers of the storms
> Steal the living heart away?
>
> Greek avengers used to cry
> Of three women in the air.
> Deaf to that religion, I
> Leave my barren house and seek
> Forces of my own to speak
> Simple reasons for despair.
>
> Waiting for the rain to fall,
> Waiting for the air to slice
> Lilies' heads along the wall;
> What have I to do with such,
> Whether they be here or gone?
> Let them tumble at a touch,
> Continents, suck up the sea,
> Level a blind mountain down;
> Let me alone, let me alone.

49

Joyce's "I Hear an Army" (*Chamber Music*). Probably his finest poem:

> I hear an army charging upon the land
> And the thunder of horses plunging, foam about their knees.
> Arrogant, in black armour, behind them stand,
> Disdaining the reins, with fluttering whips, the charioteers.
>
> They cry unto the night their battle name:
> I moan in sleep when I hear from afar their whirling laughter.
> They cleave the gloom of dreams, a blinding flame.
> Clanging, clanging upon the heart as upon an anvil.
>
> They come shaking in triumph their long green hair:
> They come out of the sea and run shouting by the shore.
> My heart, have you no wisdom thus to despair?
> My love, my love, my love, why have you left me alone?

I think, too—always—of Lincoln's beautifully cadenced sentence:

> To His care commending you, as I hope in your prayers you will commend me . . .

To me the most poignant short story published in America in the last few years is Truman Capote's "A Christmas Memory"—the story of seven-year-old Buddy and his sixty-year-old cousin whom he calls his friend. They gather firewood together, spend their saved pennies for spices, fruits, and nuts, bake their first fruitcakes together, and each makes the other a kite for Christmas. When this memoir first appeared, the reviewers who mentioned the story at all praised it for the vividness of its atmosphere—the fragrance of fruitcakes baking in the old kitchen stove, etc. Not one of them spoke of the last paragraph, wherein the art resides. The last lines can't be read without tears:

This is our last Christmas together.

Life separates us . . . I have a new home. But it doesn't count. Home is where my friend is, and there I never go.

But . . . a morning arrives in November, a leafless birdless coming of winter morning, when she cannot rouse herself to exclaim: "Oh my, it's fruitcake weather."

And when that happens I know it. A message saying so merely confirms a piece of news that some secret vein had already received, severing from me an irreparable part of myself, letting it loose like a kite on a broken string. That is why, walking across a school campus on this particular December morning, I keep searching the sky. As if I expected to see, rather like hearts, a lost pair of kites hurrying toward heaven.

The consummate art of the last sentence! Even the punctuation contributes: the period after "sky." A comma or a semicolon wouldn't have sustained the emotion so well.

But there is something else to be said about the tears of Art. There exists another kind of emotion, so deep that you are too moved to weep, an "aesthetic apprehension that produces a stasis, not a kinesis": your heart is paralyzed. The best example I know is in Isak Dinesen's *Out of Africa*. She imagines a story about Christ's second coming to the earth, and she tells it in seventy-one words. With one exception, I think it is the most moving story ever told:

When the Millennium had been going on for some time, and joy was universal, Christ one evening said to Peter that He wanted, when everything was quiet, to go out for a short walk with him alone.

"Where do you want to go, my Lord?" Peter asked. "I should like," answered the Lord, "just to take a walk from the Praetorium, along that long road, up to the Hill of Calvary."

This marvel has been abominably translated:

Quand le retour du Christ eut été fêté plusieures jours, le Christ un soir dit à Pierre qu'il aimerait aller se promener, quand tout le monde seraient couchée.

"Où voulez-vous aller, Seigneur?" demanda Pierre.

"Simplement du Protoire jusqu'au Golgotha," dit le Christ, "je voudrais remonter cette côte."

The facts are given; the emotion, as if deliberately, is drained away. Why the translator left out the poignant *short* walk, *along* that *long* road; and why she had to put the populace *to bed* remains inexplicable.

Third Category—Musical Reward

In Chapter 38 of Hemingway's *A Farewell to Arms*: the recurring mountain, lake, valley, plain. I have italicized their repetition—hypnotizing orchestration:

In front of the house where we lived the *mountain* went down steeply to the little *plain* along the *lake* and we sat on the porch of the house in the sun and saw the winding of the road down the *mountain*side and the terraced vineyards on the side of the lower *mountain*, the vines all dead now for the winter and the fields divided by stone walls, and below the vineyards the houses of the town on the narrow *plain* along the *lake* shore. There was an island with two trees on the *lake* and the trees looked like the double sails of a fishing boat. The *mountains* were sharp and steep on the other side of the *lake* and down at the end of the *lake* was the *plain* of the Rhone *Valley* flat between the two ranges of *mountains;* and up the *valley* where the *mountains* cut it off was the Dent du Midi. It was a high snowy *mountain* and it dominated the *valley* but it was so far away that it did not make a shadow.

From De Quincy's "Suspiria." In all literature this is one of the greatest gems of rhythmic prose:

And her eyes if they were seen would be neither sweet nor subtle; no man could read their story; they would be found filled
with perishing dreams and with wrecks of forgotten delirium.

Walter Savage Landor:

There are no voices that are not soon mute, there is no name,
with whatever emphasis of passionate love repeated, of which
the echoes are not faint at last.

Daphne du Maurier:

. . . The pleasure and pain of love, once breathed upon the air,
rose but to fall again, like blossoms or like rain, infecting all
things living with pain and ecstasy.

Joyce's *Portrait of the Artist as a Young Man*:

In the soft grey silence he could hear the bump of the balls; and
from here and there through the quiet air the sound of the
cricket bats; pick, pack, pock, puck: like drops of water in a
fountain falling softly in the brimming bowl.

Nothing in the last years (with the exception of the ghastly
poetry published in the *Paris Review* and most other magazines)
has enraged me more than Dudley Fitts's translation of the
poems from the Greek Anthology. As an example I offer his
rendering of the beautiful Kallimachos elegy, "They told me
Heraclitus, they told me you were dead." He regards the William Johnson Cory translation as "salon versifying" and changes

. . . A handful of grey ashes long, long ago at rest,
Still are thy pleasant voices, thy nightingales awake;
For Death, he taketh all away, but these he cannot take.

to the following:

And you are ashes now, old friend from Halikarnaso.
Ashes now:
    but your nightingale songs live on,

And Death, the destroyer of every lovely thing,
Shall not touch them with his blind all-cancelling fingers.

Only one good line. And I wonder why he thought it a good idea to use a mental adjective like "all-cancelling" fingers in the translation of poetry. The translators of the new Modern Bible should have used the talent of this adulterator.

Soon after the appearance of the new Biblical translation, a teacher told me of its effect upon children. She said that if you read the St. James version to them, they listen spellbound. Not really understanding the words, they are magnetized by the poetry. But when you read them the new version they don't listen at all, no spell exists to hold them captive.

Fourth Category—Mental Reward

Cocteau's "Portraits-Souvenir." I quote the passage in translation because for some reason it is more striking in English than in French. (And in the original there is no mention of "bruised proud knees"—if I remember correctly):

> Imagine the havoc that could be created by Dargeles . . . with his night-black lock of hair, half-closed eyes and bruised proud knees on grubs like us, desperate for love, unaware of the enigma of the senses and possessing the least protection in the world against that terrible damage caused to every sensitive heart by the supernatural sexuality of beauty.

All is rewarding, but especially the last phrase—a category of beauty uniquely defined.

Another example—Rebecca West's *The Fountain Overflows:*

> My mother could not speak to strangers except with such naïveté that they thought her a simpleton, or with such subtlety that they thought her mad. She was never much more negotiable than William Blake.

or

> Yet when people had passed a certain threshold in the lives of either papa or mama, which they did easily enough by attaining a high pitch of desolation, both were able to exercise on behalf of the desolate a celestial form of cunning nearly irresistible. They were as tricky as a couple of winged foxes.

Henry James, in *Travelling Companions:*

> I had served his purpose, and had already passed into that limbo of unhonoured victims, the experience—intellectual and other—of genius.

Cyril Connolly, in *The Unquiet Grave:*

> In my religion there would be no exclusive doctrine; all would be love, poetry and doubt. Life would be sacred, because it is all we have, and death our common denominator, the fountain of consideration.

Sybille Bedford, in *The Legacy:*

> She faced the company with easy, absent animation . . . Her look turned inward again, as if to meet a memory.

Monica Stirling, "Love in the Third Person" (*Journeys We Shall Never Make*):

> She's one of those people who can create a universe in other people's imagination.

Ben Hecht, in a symposium on "Men and Love":

> Of all the worlds in which a man lives, the most difficult for him to understand—and remember—is the world of love. Cold is the memory of love, colder than all other memories. Remember amour—and it is death you see, not love. Your heart kneels at many graves, and where you have loved most wildly the silence is deepest.

Proust, in *Remembrance of Things Past:*

> But is it not the fact . . . that art . . . makes the man himself
> apparent, rendering externally visible . . . that intimate com-
> position of those worlds which we call individual persons and
> which, without the aid of art, we would never know?

And finally, a superlative example of the kind of writing
that "seizes and holds captive the mind" . . . the writing of a
person who inhabits a mysterious personal universe—Isak Dinesen, "Shadows on the Grass":

> For we have in the dream forsaken our allegiance to the orga-
> nizing, controlling and rectifying forces of the world, the uni-
> versal Conscience. We have sworn fealty to the wild, incalculable
> creative forces, the Imagination of the universe.

. . . a paragraph that explodes stunningly upon the mind, and
then upon the imagination.

This phrase is Auden's and, I believe, of Yeats before him.

"No, please don't ask me to go, I can't listen to a harpsichord concert, even when played by Landowska."
"Why not?"
"Because I don't like the harpsichord."
"Why not?"
"For the best of all reasons. Because it's not a piano."
The great music written for the piano and beautifully played by the great pianists has been my life's delirium, and I can say with Sir Herbert Read that "my profoundest experience has been, not religious, not moral, but aesthetic."

Chicago 1913. On a Sunday afternoon, a few months before I started the *Little Review,* I went to a Paderewski concert in Orchestra Hall. Afterward I walked triumphantly along Michigan Boulevard and vowed to become a great pianist. But as I began to say the words, taking the solemn oath, I stopped. How dared I go on, knowing as I did that I would never become a real pianist—I hadn't the stamina, the courage, the patience or the discipline for such a labourious miracle. Besides, I already had two aims in life, two passions: I loved ideas almost as much as I loved music. A magazine devoted to art and ideas would satisfy both needs, and this, I was sure, I could accomplish.

To create a *Little Review* serving both art and the mind (I thought I had a mind, and knew I had the *nature* of an artist) would demand no stamina, courage, or discipline. Patience? Impatience would be an advantage, and I had plenty of that.

Thus began my career as an amateur—an amateurism so intense that it has served me as a profession and allowed me to regard myself ever after as that person who could easily (if only slightly stronger) have become the lyric pianist she longed to be.

Of course, since I have as much faith in my common sense as I have pleasure in my illusions, I realized that I had better find a way to justify my position. I searched and searched for a life motto and finally found a perfect one: "As if . . ." (Tamquam si . . .)

Since that decisive afternoon in Chicago, though my parents continued to believe that I would become a great pianist, I knew where I stood: my "as if" megalomania gave me the vicarious experience of the artist's ecstasy without having had to undergo the daily lonely labour of the functioning virtuoso. I have been a cheat, and no one has ever been more rewarded for cheating. I have ignored Orage's admonition: "Remember you're a pianist, not a piano." I have not acted upon the piano, I have been acted upon *by* the piano.

My aesthetic delirium has been expended chiefly upon the piano music of the great romantics. I have never loved Mozart, never been able to feel the "celestial" quality of his music; in fact I actively dislike much of it. I flee the opening measures of his "Haffner" or "Jupiter" symphonies as I would flee a person who began talking to me in a strident, insistent voice. There is a certain blaring boisterousness in certain classics that I want to avoid; there is no healing or ineffable beauty for me in music that blurts out its intentions too aggressively—I want to say, "Please let me alone." Also, I find no emotional sustenance in Scarlatti or Haydn, etc., nor has Beethoven been among my gods except for his three or four "entirely beautiful" master-pieces—which I won't name, thereby inviting antagonism. His "Prometheus Overture," his Eighth Symphony—oh dear, how can one listen? Bach . . . of course, but all the great things, not those the musicologists choose. I *cannot* listen to the "Goldbergs" or the "Brandenburgs."

I have no rapport (like Einstein's) with the music to which one nods one's head or taps one's foot; and it never occurs to me to listen to the gay or the ponderous. I avoid programs praised by the musicologists; their musical choices are as wearisome to me as their dry, lisping, aged voices. I rarely listen to chamber music—I'm too impatient for "something to happen." "What?" "Something more. "More *what*? Surely you can indicate something." "Something that makes your heart stand still; those moments of great stillness which arrive when Art 'occurs'."

Cocteau said that the music you listen to with head-in-hands is suspect. I couldn't disagree more.

One reason I could never become a professional pianist is that I would practise only the music I consider utterly beautiful and for which I have a deathless love—the music of love and death. This is the music I know I shall ask to hear when I am dying; this is the music that produces the emotion of head-in-hands, and it is this emotion which lures people into churches —the need to feel (for at least a few weekly moments) an intimation of the sublime. I have gone to church rarely in my life, but I remember a Sunday night in Dr. Percy Stickney Grant's Fifth Avenue and Twelfth Street church in New York when I looked up at the inscription over the altar: "Do this in remembrance of Me" . . . You have to put your head in your hands or everyone will see that you are crying.

———

I have never had to listen twice to a piece of music before knowing whether I love it or not. I cannot *learn* to love or like things; music is always a matter of coup de foudre or the opposite for me. In my life there is no place for the in-between, and I always ask my friends never to buy records for me without

59

first asking if I want them. I select musical items as I select
books, and the other day I ran through a catalogue of 500 book
titles, of which only fifteen or twenty would have interested me.

My musical standards are the ineffable and the lyrical, and
my choice of recordings is limited to those disques which are
ineffably and lyrically played. By "ineffable" I mean that state
of Art which produces a certain kind of awe: the inexpressible
somehow expressed, but held within its own mystery, available
to those who are as sensitized to the composer's magnetic field
as is the composer himself. By "lyrical" I mean that which can
be defined as an affinity between the "breathing out and breathing in" of the performer's organism and my own. Often I can't
say more in criticizing a pianist than that he "breathes wrong."
How justify such a criterion? Rather easily, I suppose; by
reasoning, by proving, that the rhythmic breathing of an art-
emotion is based on the breathing rhythm of an artist rather
than on that of a businessman or a scientist, of a professor, a
mechanic, a butcher, or a simple bourgeois. I can think of many
simple examples. For instance, I can produce "entirely beautiful" capital M's—like this:

But when *The Fiery Fountains* appeared I saw that my publisher
and friend, Gorham Munson, had asked his book designer to
decorate the pages with some small M.A.'s.

"How did you like the little design?" Gorham asked me.

"My dear Gorham . . . those poor little bourgeois M's? I
loathed them."

"But why?" he asked, desolate. "I was sure you'd like them."

"Gorham!" I said, "I am *not* a member of the bourgeoisie."

Though I so easily dispense with the knowledge of the musicologist and so detest his way of talking about music, I am fascinated by the knowledge of the virtuoso and his way of talking about his craft. On this basis I edit composers and performers just as I would edit a piece of writing. Thus I protect myself and the audiences who listen to my salon concerts from the boredom of mediocre music and second-rate performers. To exhibit my predilections I identify with the great pianists, I play their recordings for my friends as if *I* were the performer; I regulate and control my electrophone, allowing no mechanical vibrations to mar the sonorities; I compare and judge the qualities of Richter, Horowitz, Janis, Rubinstein, Cziffra, Iturbi, Uninsky, Lympany, Casadesus, Anda, Rachmaninoff, Cortot, and the others*—(for some reason I haven't been able to find the Gilels and Ashkenazy disques I want) as if I understood their genius better than any music critic does. As an impresario I consider myself infallible, and no one ever listens to my programs without saying afterward, "You always play music that I want to hear over and over."

I have made a list of piano recordings which I consider "gems" to be played over and over without losing for a second the listeners' attention. My definition of a gem? A great or small masterpiece which transports you from the daily world in which you live to a monde à côté—a quite other world, next door but removed from all earthly concerns; a world in which you are for a moment unconscious of everything outside it.

I don't know how to describe the rapture that fills me when, having discovered a new gem, I can play it for my friends. If they are far away I think at once of taking a train, though I have no money for trains; or of driving to Paris, which

---

* And now (later) the unique Alicia de Larrocha. And Martha Argerich.

takes even more money and a day longer, while I worry about the uncontrollable impatience of my waiting audience. Of course I could mail the disque to them, but oh, not to be there when they hear it for the first time! I suppose our immeasurable shared pleasure comes from the electric current passing through the salon as we listen together to some pianist magician evoking our brief longing and our "perishing dreams."

My list of gem recordings extends as far back as 1925, and it isn't a long list because gems in my terms are rare. Sometimes I wait for six months before finding a new one to add to my collection. Once chosen, I play it night and day in an obsession which lasts, usually, about a month. Then another discovery moves into first place and a new obsession begins—but without challenging the memory of the former one. I have never chosen a gem that has lost its status to me, and I am always astonished at how often a musical gem differs from an ordinary performance by a simple difference in tempo. Which is more important —tempo or tone? This is like the old question of line *or* colour. I always decided, with Blake, that line was paramount—therefore he couldn't accuse me of cowardice. But how choose *tempo* over *tone* in music? After all, the elements of time and tempo exist in drums, in tomtoms; tone is requisite in melody (music of the spheres?). It is Cortot's tempo in César Franck's "Symphonic Variations" that sets his recording above others; or Toscanini's and Horowitz's in the Tschaikowsky Piano Concerto. As to tone, I never care to listen to Serkin: he hasn't the tonal resonances of the great new pianists.

I have decided that a wrong tempo disturbs me even more than a lack of beautiful tone.

Tempo. I had a most satisfying dream:

Rachmaninoff was playing with orchestra in Carnegie Hall. He was so troubled by the conductor's slow tempo, and finally so enraged, that he left the piano, grabbed the conductor by the collar, lifted him off his feet, hoisted him off the stage and deposited him in the wings. Then, smiling, he walked back to the piano, sat down, lifted his arm en conducteur, and, leading the orchestra as he played, exhibited the effect of a proper tempo on music otherwise reduced to banality. I wakened from this exhilarating dream to the audience's cries of "Bravo!"

Here is a partial list of my chosen recordings which I guarantee will not only hold my listeners' attention, but hypnotize them into the "state of art" as they pass from one world into another.

I always begin my concerts with five short pieces played by Moura Lympany, as the best introduction to the mood necessary for the art-state into which I wish to lure my audience.

Examining my titles, of course someone will say scornfully, "Oh! So you play only 'salon music!'." "Of course," I will answer, "exactly that, which is just what I want: a salon program of salon music played in a salon and enjoyed by a salon audience." In such music there's always the element of what Time has endorsed as a prevailing, a permanent Art verdict: the verdict of charisma (as in all realms)—"De gustibus non est disputandum." No dry, used-up, or transient music has ever found its way into this category. (The great public has realized, has decided, that Frost's "Stopping by woods on a snowy evening" is his most beautiful poem. There's no reason to deride this universal recognition, in poetry or in music, or to imagine that it can be changed.)

Anyone who wants to can offer his audience an hour of Bartók or Hindemith or any of the others at their most tiresome, but I shall never do it. I echo Casals' opinion that modern music is an error.

Herewith my concert programs, arranged not necessarily in order of evaluation but of contrast:

63

MOURA LYMPANY—"Famous Classics for the Piano" (Angel).
I play the first five pieces straight through, as they stand:
Debussy—"Clair de Lune"
Liszt—"Valse Impromptu"
Chopin—"Preludes, Nos. 7 and 20 (opus 28)
Granados—"The Maiden and the Nightingale"
(Side two) Brahms—Intermezzo No. 2 (opus 117)
(Details later.)
ITURBI—"Allegro de Concert de Granados" (Columbia). (Details later.)

(Here I must interrupt my list to include my discovery of *ALICIA DE LARROCHA* [in her] Granados "Goyescas.") I would be willing to risk my critical reputation (if I had one) by saying that I consider her "Los Requiebros" the greatest piece of piano playing of our century. Second on the recording, to me, comes "Epilogo (Allegro appassionato–Andantino spianato)." (Details later.)

Bach—"Chorale: 'I Call upon Thee, Jesus' ", orchestrated and conducted by STOKOWSKI" (Victor). I have had this recording since 1930 and often think that it is the most beautiful objective music ever written. It is the music of consolation and is less moving on the piano or the harpsichord.
HOROWITZ—"Two Scriabin Etudes, No. 7 (opus 9) and No. 5 (opus 42)" (Victor). He played them in his Carnegie Hall concert on February 25, 1953. The first is a lyrical gem; the second a rage of grief or of love. Both incomparably played.
HAROLD BAUER AND OSSIP GABRILOWITSCH—"Arensky's Waltz for two pianos" (RCA). This recording was made in 1929 and, as Harold Schonberg has said, "A lovelier piano disque has never been made." The finesse with which the two pianists handle the rhythms is almost startling.
On this same recording Rachmaninoff plays fragments of the Schumann "Carnaval" with an élan, a style that make all other recordings sound flaccid. Really Rachmaninoff was the most élégant of all pianists.
RICHTER—"Six Rachmaninoff Preludes" (Deutsche Grammophon). First I play No. 5 because no one else has played this Prelude with such originality—the theme at the end quickened

to an amazing tempo. If there is time I also play No. 1 (opus 23).

Lympany has done the entire twenty-four, and my favourites are Nos. 6, 8 and 9 (opus 23). Beautiful.

CZIFFRA—"César Franck's Variations Symphoniques" (Voix de son Maître). Conducted by André Vandermoot. This recording doesn't compare with the Cortot performance of 1934. I slip quietly from the opening theme to the middle section—the lovely sustained passage which begins just seven minutes after the opening. Cortot's tempo was slightly faster, his mood more *still*, and consequently more enthralling. Cziffra's cadenza doesn't exist in comparison. Philip Entremont's interpretation breaks up the structure rather badly.

RUBINSTEIN—"Poulenc's Intermezzo in A flat, and Ravel's 'La Vallée des Cloches'" (RCA). The first is an exquisite trifle, adorable; the second extraordinary—and I'm sure that no one else has ever struck such a bell-like tone, on one note; it's as if the piano had suddenly become another instrument. In the Gieseking recording this note is almost inaudible.

LYMPANY—"Rachmaninoff's First Piano Concerto" (Voix de son Maître). I do only a bit of the first movement, since the ravishing theme is so familiar, and then I slide into the Andante which is not only poignant but spellbinding, and seems to be made to Lympany's measure. The loveliest moment comes in the perfection of her feathery passage near the end of this movement. (Janis does this passage in a rather choppy way.) For my salon concerts I don't play the third movement.

UNINSKY—"The twenty-four Chopin Etudes" (Philips). I've found these better than any others so far. Played with admirable grace, charm, lack of exaggeration. Cziffra has played them with distortions—a little too Hungarian perhaps? For my audience I play my favourite No. 10 (opus 10), and Nos. 1 and 3 (opus 25). I dislike the way Janis plays No. 3.

CASADESUS—"Ravel's 'Ondine'" (CBS). I've heard that this is the interpretation Ravel preferred. It is superior to Gieseking's and seemingly flawless—though isn't there, once or twice, a slight blurring of design?

GEZA ANDA—"Schumann's 'Etudes Symphoniques'" (Deutsche Grammophon). Anda is better here than in some of his Chopin

Preludes, in which one can often hear him *striking* the chords. The Myra Hess version, though very beautiful in depth of tone, has moments of almost ponderous slowness. I begin with Variation No. 3, follow it with No. 4; then the two posthumous Variations, both lovely and never before recorded. I end with Variation No. 11. Our favourite pianist, Allen Tanner, played this music better than anyone, we always thought.

KHACHATURIAN's Valse from the "Masquerade Suite," and "Romance" conducted by ALFRED NEWMAN (Capitol). The first captivating; the second, with its trumpet solo, touching.

RICHTER—"Liszt's Valse Oubliée, No. 2" (Philips). This is a trouvaille, uniquely played.

LYMPANY and JANIS—"Prokofiev's Piano Concerto No. 1 (Angel), and No. 3" (Mercury). I play just a bit of one or the other on my program. Janis is stunning; Lympany makes Prokofiev almost lyrical.

And then, as a contrast to Prokofiev's violence, I end my concert with the most poignant little "song" ever written—Schubert's "Deutsche Tanza" No. 7, (opus 33) played by two pianists, VITYA VRONSKY and VICTOR BABIN (Decca). I *think* this melody was used as a song by the schoolboy choir in that old German film "The Unfinished Symphony." It moves my audience almost to tears.

If urged, I am only too happy to continue and I present two singers. I almost never buy voice records because there are so many singers with "made" voices who don't sing simple songs simply enough to make them "gems" in my terms. No amount of musicianship can reconcile me to this failing. Three great exceptions are the voices of CLAUDIA MUZIO, MARGUERITE D'ALVAREZ, and MAGGIE TEYTE—and of course MARY GARDEN and GEORGETTE (though the latter's recordings of Debussy, Duparc, Reynaldo Hahn, and others were lost in the Columbia factory fire, years ago in New York).

I begin with Teyte's "Chanson Triste." Duparc. (Victor Red Seal). What charm! What exquisite musicianship!

66

Then D'Alvarez's beautiful, phenomenal voice in "Do not go, my love, without asking my leave." Hageman.

Next, Muzio's "Spirate Pur, Spirate." Donaudy. (Columbia). For voice as voice, and phrasing as phrasing, I know no one more perfect than Muzio. I'm not interested in her opera recordings—but then I don't buy opera disques.

For my climax, the most heartrending of all the songs that Muzio sang: "O Del Mio Amato Ben." Donaudy. (Columbia).

Last summer I played this program for three American friends—wife, husband and daughter; not musicians, but people who are moved by the things that move me. The program lasted for three hours. My audience sat without speaking, except to say, "Please go on," or "Please play that again." The next day I drove to Antibes to say goodbye—they were leaving for New York the following morning. "We have a favour to ask. Let's drive back to Cannet in the two cars, and will you play again everything you played yesterday?"

This time they stayed for four hours, and during that time not one of them changed his chair or his position, saying nothing but "How beautiful!" or "Do it once more." Not one of them asked for a cigarette or a drink. We had all forgotten that we were in a world where cocktails are available and enjoyable.

Such an audience gave me time for an extra finale, so I played the Adagio of Rachmaninoff's Second Symphony, which is of a sustained beauty that lingers with you for days. I have Kurt Sanderling's conducting (Deutsche Grammophon), but I prefer the old Rodzinsky recording—though for some reason its re-issue is inferior, and one measure (the most touching in the whole movement) has been omitted. I don't play the first, second, and fourth movements.

For this four hour concert I also had time for BYRON JANIS: Liszt's "Sonnet de Pétrarque," No. 104 (Mercury).

67

Résumé. Of all the disques I have collected during the last few years, there are two that I play more often than others, that I listen to with endless, undiminished delight and satisfaction; two pianists—not among the newest—who especially meet my perfectionist standards: José Iturbi, whose playing I have known for years, and Moura Lympany, of whom I knew nothing until I was sent one of her recordings.

ITURBI. The Granados "Allegro de Concert"—dramatic and very moving. He plays it without ostentation, neither underscoring its brilliance nor sentimentalizing the keenness and pain of its "little phrase." His performance is rapt, and concentrated, and controlled, therefore "musical." The distinguishing features of his pianism are his incisiveness, his enunciation, his particular accentuation. Nothing illustrates these qualities better than the "different" way he plays the Grieg Concerto. I have records of this concerto by all the great pianists and they all play it alike —except Iturbi. Of course there are slight differences between Rubinstein's and Gieseking's performances, between Hess's and Novaes's and Arrau's, etc.; but since they all play the melodic themes with the appropriate "loveliness," audiences ask for nothing more. I'm talking about basic differences, and with Iturbi the whole conception is different because of that special individual accent, incision, and race which dictate his tempos and rhythms. He plays and conducts the orchestra at the same time, and his minute, definite distinctions give the concerto a style, a finesse, which other pianists miss. I don't know whether I'm right in attributing this difference to dynamics, but it seems to me so vital a distinction (and so vitally a dilettante's concern) that I don't understand why other pianists don't profit by listening to him. In the same way, I don't understand why all pianists don't play Rachmaninoff's Second Piano Concerto with the basic structures and tempos which the composer imposed. A young French pianist, Gabriel Tacchino, does, and Lympany does; but Richter doesn't. He reduces Rachmaninoff's lyricism by a too slow tempo, and you don't long to pace up and down the room as you do when Rachmaninoff soars into his climaxes; you sit still and almost inattentive because Richter allows you to do so. I feel sad about it, but Richter has begun to disappoint me; his programs are so unenthralling.

LYMPANY. One of the landmarks in my musical life has been the discovery of Lympany's "completely beautiful" playing. I knew at once, as she began the Debussy "Clair de Lune," that no one had ever played it so exactly in the right mood for me, the right breathing. Later, when I played it for Solita and our great friend Elizabeth Clark, Solita borrowed Gurdjieff's terminology to express what she felt: "She plays with honour." And Elizabeth said: "She plays running passages in a special rippling, murmurous way. You never hear her hit the keys; she melts them, but each note is heard clearly. She has a special genius for softening the end of a moving phrase, and the delicately suggested rubato she employs in doing so is beyond description."

I know at least twenty recordings of this exquisite reverie, but I cling to Lympany's in spite of two minor reservations. First, I prefer Iturbi's lighter, swifter, running bass—no one else plays it quite so simply, reducing its importance, making it more flowing; second, I applaud his sonorous accenting (near the end) of the one important note, ignored entirely by Gieseking and others, though called for by the musical notation. Lympany stresses it, of course, but without such resonance. What is less good in Iturbi's conception is his opening tempo, a little too fast, lacking the hush and mystery of Lympany's beginning. Again a question of breathing. John Ciardi said, "Art is the way the mind breathes." Not at all, I say; art is the way the solar plexus breathes. Richter doesn't breathe "right" at all in this piece; he obviously doesn't know the mood of moonlight.

Nearly all of Lympany's conceptions (I don't know her Bach) are marked by a rare responsiveness to great lyrical music.

She often leaves an almost imperceptible pause between the last note of one measure of a melodic phrase and its connection with the first note of the next measure. Thus the lovely undulations of her playing depend on the marvelous continuation she manages to sustain even during pauses . . . ("The phasing out and the blending in that make for tonal drama"—Irving Kolodin; so I can say "that make for tonal piano playing.") All this can be heard especially in her Chopin Nocturne, No. 13, in which Rubinstein's climax is so disappointing.

In her playing of the two shortest Chopin Preludes (opus 28)—No. 7 and No. 20 (the twelve great measures)—she is unique in the first one, as far as I know. I've read somewhere that Chopin conceived this Prelude as a little dance (though I don't believe it). Geza Anda plays it as a rather gay little dance, but Lympany considers it a little sorrow and makes it heartbreaking.

As to her No. 20, I was so moved the first time I heard it that I wrote to her, telling about my experience with this Prelude* and asking if she had ever imagined playing it a little slower. She answered: "It is interesting that you mention the tempo of the Prelude. I did actually play it slower, but the recorders felt that it dragged on record—so I did it faster." This not only touched me but made me laugh—as if it was the easiest thing in the world to put one's self under the control of engineers.

Cortot played No. 20 as a strong, too loud funeral procession, and crashed out the last chord (thirteenth measure) in the most brutal way, with no "lonely depths of feeling."

April, 1968. A new disque—the only gem I've discovered this year: ALICIA DE LARROCHA's recording of the Granados "Goyescas." It has overwhelmed me.

---

* Page 171.

What power, what delicacy, what emotional depth and energy of temperament! I played first the "Epilogo" (Face 4) and found her phrasings of its themes so poignant that my neck became too weak to support my head, which wanted to sink down over my right shoulder as if the weight of such beautiful playing was too much to bear without fainting. Then I played "Los Requiebros" (Face 1), a requiem, a hymn of "rest in peace." At the first playing it didn't sound like a requiem to me; at the second, I realized that it was exactly the kind of requiem I myself would have composed had I been a musician—music that isn't all sorrow because it also holds an element of defiant rejoicing: the beloved has died, but the "presence of that absence" is still with you, as it will always be, forever. De Larrocha's every nuance, every rubato, conveys this understanding, underscores it; and no one else could play this requiem as she does. You feel that she loves the music of Granados as one loves one person above all others, and it is her conception and execution, plus the extraordinary beauty of the music, which explain why I consider this disque the finest pianism of our time.

At first—having heard her only once, on radio—I had expected to admire most her astounding virtuosity; but now I found that what moved me above all—how say it simply?—is that she "has a way" with a melody; she plays it as if she were writing a poem. It is her *phasing out and blending in* that produce the special, double commemoration I mentioned, and as I listened to all this expenditure of genius I was led into the most extravagant fantasies. I imagined that I was having a conversation with this prodigious Spanish virtuoso and I said, "What would you answer if someone asked whether you could play on the piano—imagine it!—a melody as simple as 'Annie Laurie'?" "Ah," she says, "of course I can play this beautiful little song." So I listen to her playing it; I feel her right hand moulding the rhythms of the poem, listen to the pauses between her

71

phrasings, and revel in the Granados accompaniment she invents for them.

The other day on my transistor, I happened to hear one of Granados' own recordings of "The Maiden and the Nightingale." Curious, disconcerting; the most rigidly masculine playing I've ever listened to, not a single nuance—pure, simple virility. It's also disconcerting to hear that De Larrocha wants to become known "more internationally" by reviving all the old classic repertoire—Mozart and the others who should be none of her business, just as Spain's music is not the business of Anglo-Saxon virtuosos. Nevertheless, I should love to hear what she would do with Chopin's Etude No. 10 (opus 10), which Iturbi has said he considers unplayable; with Scriabin's "Poème No. 2" (opus 32), and Liszt's "Sonetto del Petrarca," No. 104.

Not long ago I wrote to her, expressing my appreciation of her uniqueness. She answered:

> Thank you very much for your kind letter, and I am very touched for the praise you dedicate to me in your book which will be published nearly. But I confess you that I am the conviction that everybody having musicality, rithm, and sensibility (the basis of all kind of music) can play the Spanish music. In my case, the Spanish Music is only a little part of my repetory, which always has been Universal, containing all piano music styles.

How modest, and how wrong, she is. Musicality, rhythm, and sensibility are the requisites of all good piano playing, but they don't always, or even often, guarantee genius.

I have found (according to my standards) only one flaw in De Larrocha's musicality. It occurs at the end of the "Epilogo." Through several measures she fails to fulfill my idea of the almost imperceptible pause I so love between the last note of one measure as it merges into the first note of the next measure. This phenomenon has perhaps become an obsession with me, but my breathing so insists on it that when it doesn't occur I feel a little troubled, startled, impatient, regretful, and quite sad . . . as if I were listening to bad pedalling. I wonder if this great pianist would find any sense in what I've said.

A little later, 1968. And now another gem—on my transistor. It's hard to believe that another would arrive so soon, but MARTHA ARGERICH is also a genius of temperament. Though I remember Orage's definition of temperament as "lack of decision," I still enjoy using the word as we have always used it, meaning predominance of decision, especially in the sense of flame and frenzy. Argerich plays the Prokofiev Third Piano Concerto with sharper precision than almost anyone, combining the fire of her nature with a tenderness that is surprising. No other interpreter of Prokofiev has found so many places, so many justifications, for pianissimos in his music. She also plays one of the Chopin Revolutionary Etudes astoundingly. But I have been disappointed in her other disques—or, rather, in her selections of what music to record; the Chopin Concertos don't belong in my category of gems to be played over and over forever. To me they have been fully used, or over-used.

Argerich is only twenty-seven and is certain to be one of the giants of tomorrow.

A Digression

I have sat still all day. Except for a light lunch and an even lighter dinner, I've not moved from my favourite armchair —my "thinking" chair. My preoccupation has been an old subject, one I've never tried to formulate clearly; but this morning I had a moment of conviction that if I try hard enough I can become articulate.

The thing to do is to begin with a story—something that happened the other day and that always happens whenever I allow myself to be swept into the whirlpools of sociability. I went with some friends to see some other friends—a well-known writer whom I much admire and three other charming per-

73

sonalities, all of whom are entertaining talkers. Nothing that was said was without a certain interest to me, so why did I leave the party feeling undernourished and despondent? (As Dr. Johnson said, "There was much talk but no conversation—there was nothing discussed.")

In other words, the talk had been reportorial, not creative; meaning that it was of the *outside,* not the *inside*—the reporting of outer events instead of inner emotions. This journalistic reporting of concrete public facts on which the world thrives offers little of interest to me: I look upon it as the difference between reality and art; it is the void that exists between complete and incomplete people, and what I want to do is to define "complete."

There is something luxuriant about complete people. Their conversation shuns reportorial information, consists instead of *personal information.* Personal richness is the only kind of communication that contributes radiance, that can hold the attention of an inspired listener, and that eliminates depression. Simplicity (real), naturalness, abundance, weight.

In *Little Review* days we used to say that the only conversation worth listening to was about general ideas. We meant the ideas of psychology, and especially in one realm: the degree of personal accretions which certain people possess and make you aware of. We used to make a game of this phenomenon: we would ask someone to walk across the room two or three times, and then we would all try to evaluate that person's essence. Was it a dry, thin essence? Was it like a fruit with much juice? And so on.

In reportorial communication there is always a feeling of competition. About what? About showing off one's knowledge. With complete people you never feel this scurrying to say something that will outshine the other talkers. With the scurriers you are deprived of the restfulness and new energy which accumulates when great talkers are revealing the underlayers of their inner lives, demonstrating that what they say comes from their completeness as special, original, human beings.

The other day, as my chattering friends continued their reports of what was happening outside of them, I longed to ask, "What has been happening IN you? Why don't you tell me something about yourselves that will absorb me, make me question you in the hope of hearing what experiences have filled your days and nights, what you've been finding out about yourself and others, what personal conflicts have undone you, or have you emerged from them unscathed? What *whole* experiences have you had?" In such gatherings it is almost certain that there will have been no "whole" experiences to relate. People today have little time, inclination, or capacity for them.

Whole experiences often happen to very simple people; they are always happening to artists, and they never happen to incomplete people. When you're talking with the latter you feel that they don't exist as people at all; and with them *you* don't exist as a person. It's dehumanizing, you feel stripped of life, you cease to be a human being, you are treated as if you were a "fluff of migratory thistledown."*

I find the conversation—the writing—of music critics largely reportorial. They instruct you. (I too am being instructive? I suppose so, but. . . .) Critics tell you how the music was written, how the pianist plays it—his degree of virtuosity, his "steel" fingers, his "golden tone," etc.; all of which you can hear for yourself and don't need to be told. They never get down to *under*-knowledge of what is going on, they never speculate as to why one pianist's "being" makes his playing deeper, more sensitive, more poignant, more alluring, more savage, more desolate or more reverent than another's. They don't say, "This man (or woman) must have known real love, this one has been

---

* Dorothy Caruso.

75

heartbroken, this one has known only romantic love, this one must surely have experienced unrequited love, this one seems to have had no great emotions at all." I feel sure that I have *heard* the personal information revealed in the playing, but I would be interested to know whether the critics agree with me as to the source of the inspiration. That would be a conversation.

I began these "critical" notes to show what I think can be learned from human categories through the medium of Art. Though you can know little about people you don't know personally, you can imagine much about them by listening to what they reveal of themselves through their music or their poetry. Would these great pianists be "inside" or "outside" talkers?

I feel that Iturbi would be simple, spontaneous, eager, and natural—inside revelations given to any listener worthy of being talked to. Richter? Oh, very "inside"; a flood of personal talk about impersonal ideas, especially the art of piano playing. Rubinstein? Nth power personal information. Horowitz? A Russian's natural, intimate, almost childlike revelations. Ravel? More reserved, more "outside." Lympany? Rather baffling. You feel no indiscretion in deciding that there is a barrier—a space —between the woman herself and her art. You feel free to presuppose a mystery between her human and musical emotions, something perhaps as vague to her as to you. So when—a long time after seeing and hearing her play—I heard that she doesn't like to talk about her playing, I felt that fact contributing to my impression of barrier; and I imagine that people often approach her (like the man in the *New Yorker* cartoon) saying, "You don't fool me, Miss Corlis, you're a real person under that pretty face." She may accept such clowning helplessly. Perhaps I'm wrong, but my theory may account for a certain inscrutability that I feel in her, and which she might laugh at.

De Larrocha? I have such awe of her playing that I have no ideas at all about her humanity. I mean that anyone whose art emotions are as intense as hers leaves you baffled as to what her life emotions must be. You feel indiscreet—almost impertinent—if you try to speculate about them. It must be what Georgette meant when talking about her portrait-sketches of people: "I can draw any face but a loved face." I have a real emotion about De Larrocha. Therefore she must remain unknowable to me. And yet I know that she and her art must have an identical nobility.

I have known one pianist whose conversation sprang from such informality and adult disclosure that "inside" and "outside" were equally balanced in his particular personal civilization. HAROLD BAUER.

But why not write about these subtle matters more simply? Why not talk about pianists as one talks about voices?—speaking voices. There's nothing more seductive or undefinable than a beautiful speaking voice. We used to telephone Marguerite D'Alvarez just to hear her say "hello," and ask her to say it several times; just as we asked Georgette to repeat and repeat Corneille's "Saint douceur de ciel, adorables idées," never tiring of hearing the art of diction which she put into the last two words. Lympany's playing is like a voice you never tire of listening to. You are happy to know a pianist whose playing has the sorcery of limpid speech; and, for other moments, what the critics never fail to point out as "the power of a man." This is true, but as Brahms is supposed to have said of a certain pianist, she never "hurts the sounds."

A dilettante's delight. Listen to RICHTER playing the last seven chords of the Rachmaninoff Prelude (opus 32, No. 1).

Listen to SAMSON FRANÇOIS in Chopin's Etude (opus 25, No. 3). Just after the opening theme has been repeated for the third

THE LIFE OF ART

time, he plays two measures as no one else does—with a sudden velvet legato that gives you a sigh of pleasure. Three or four seconds.

Listen to RUBINSTEIN in the Ravel "Vallée des Cloches," where he strikes that amazing bell-like tone.

Listen to GYORGY CZIFFRA and the way he plays the three closing chords of the Liszt "Valse Impromptu."

For Chopin Waltzes, no one is so good as CORTOT, except (sometimes) DINU LIPATTI (Columbia). And if Rachmaninoff had played them . . . !

As for DE LARROCHA, try not to weep over the nuances and rubatos in her "Los Requiebros."

———————

I have lots of trouble today with old friends who have turned modern . . . one a pianist with whom I sometimes can't cope. One night, pleased at having been urged to play, she asked what we wanted. A naïve newcomer in the group, with a trusting look, asked for the Beethoven "Moonlight." The pianist responded by dashing into the final movement of the sonata, and when she had finished the naïve one said, "Oh I didn't mean *that,* I meant . . ." The pianist's silence cut the rest of the phrase. To help out, I said, "She thought you might enjoy the last movement." "No," said the wilting and disappointed one, "I mean the *lovely* part." Everyone waited for the pianist to respond properly, but she said, "No one can listen to *that* any more, I can't bear to play it." And she didn't.

The evening ended on this inflexible note, and, feeling slightly vengeful, I said as we left, "We're so sorry we couldn't have heard the 'Moonlight'"—almost expecting the pianist to relent: "Oh, come on back, I'll be glad to play it for you." But she didn't. Instead she gave me a tight, hard look, calculated to put me in my place.

I have another "modern" friend who often shocks me. In

our Sixty-first Street house in New York we had hung an old-fashioned painting of roses above the fireplace in the library. "Why do you keep such a painting?" she asked, trembling with distaste.

"Because it's so lovely, don't you see?"

"But it's not modern!" she cried.

Anodynes. Living as I do like a recluse, and thus having escaped the unbeautiful life of the modern world, I have also longed to escape from the blight of modern poetry. But this is difficult—there is no *Little Review* today to take a stand against poetry of the mental-contortion type. If you search for beauty in our time you will have to be satisfied with efforts like "The bottled brightness of heat/Holds queerly a spade's scratched flame" (James Dickey, "Mindore 1944," *Paris Review*).

"How do you stand it?" I ask Solita.

"I don't," she says. "When a new poet offers me a sample of what his brain is capable of—not under some compulsive torture but (imagine it!) as an exercise in enjoyment—I say, 'I'm sorry, but I can't read it.' My school is "Little lamb, who made thee"?' "

"Bravo!" I say. "Mine is 'Ah Psyche, from the regions which/Are holy land'."

Every day, today, in magazines of verse, I read "poems" like these:

Digging here in the clutter
Of clam and scallop shells, I left the detritus . . .
(Author unknown to me)

or,

Inside the varicose form of my God.
(Author unknown to me)

or,

Umbrellas

Under the rain-ripened skin
of black-blossoming fruit,
cling two seeds like eyes.
The dry stick is sprouting hands
and two up-rooted tendrils seek
toe-holds, like feet.

or,

Transcontinent

Where the cities end, the
dumps grow, the oil-can shacks
from Portland, Maine,

to Seattle. Broken
cars rust in Troy, New York,
and Cleveland Heights.

On the train, the people
eat candy bars, and watch
or fall asleep.

When they look outside and
see cars and shacks, they know
they're nearly there.

(Donald Hall, *Saturday Review*)

Is there *anyone* on earth, except these authors (and their publishers) who can say that he loves such "poems," anyone who
can be uplifted, nourished, inspired by such "emotions"? This
is "the poetry of the new imagination"?

Sometimes when *my* imagination has been deadened by
reading about city dumps and junkmen, bulldozers, trucks; the
brutal, the coarse, the common, the tawdry, the sordid; criminals,
sadists, rapists, killers . . . I take a walk in the clean air and
repeat to myself, as fast as they come leaping to my mind,
the simple lines of poets which are always in my memory, like
anodynes:

Over the long and the light summer land
Now sleeps the crimson petal, now the white
This emerald isle
Flow gently, sweet Afton
Sheep may safely graze
Horses, young horses, and the waves of the sea
Near the snow, near the sun, in the highest fields
I will arise and go now, and go to Innisfree
The trembling river runneth bright
I shall not hear the nightingale/ Sing on as if in pain
Nor image of thine eyes in any spring
Only in silent shadows and in dreams
The moon has sunk, and the Pleiades . . .
Art thou pale for weariness / Of climbing heaven
Lonely, eternal pilgrim
Entend la douce nuit qui marche
Over silvery fields and waters
Now I walk beneath the night
Then falls thy shadow, Cynara
And the dark rain falling, then as now
Et toi, que fais-tu?
My heart is an idiot
Un ombre comme toi
A grief ago
Odeur du temps
Have I forgot, my only Love, to love thee?
Blossom by blossom the spring begins
Rien n'est donc changé que vous?
Soft summer's sighing
The sky of birds, the planted stars
She walks in beauty, like the night
I arise from dreams of thee
Je n'ai jamais regardé ton regard
The sorrows of your changing face
The regions which/ Are holy land
These images of wonder
This is the wine, and this the bread
Let the west wind sleep on the lake
In my golden armor somewhere in a dark wood
I laid my head down on the vital grass

The woods are lovely, dark and deep
Bells occupy the sky
Au calme clair de lune, triste et beau
Winding across wide waters without sound
As long as starlight moved/Carefully around the earth
Silently through the skies you take your nightly path alone
Thick darkness and the insuperable sea
Between a sleep and a sleep
The world that was not comes to pass
And while our souls negotiate there
The quiet moon stands over roofs and orchards, revealing from
   afar each peaceful hill.

And sometimes, when my inner seething against the moderns is so intense that it prevents sleep, I soothe myself by
trying to remember all the musical motifs I know that are made
of four notes, like the sol-do-do-si of "Tristan." When I have
counted fifteen or twenty, have murmured the melodies over
and over to my agitated but attentive psyche, it has fallen
blissfully asleep.

Such is the beneficent influence of the life of emotions upon
the emotions of life.

I don't know why it is reprehensible to be a dilettante—at least a sympathetic and expert one. I *value* my dilettantism; I like to talk lightly about its serious aspects and seriously about its trivial aspects. What I most like to defend is its passion, its dazzling rewards, and my conviction that those serious people who disparage it are serious bores.

This conviction has just been revived by reading a book about Ezra Pound. Before his arrest and imprisonment, as a traitor, in a Washington insane asylum—a charge of such nonsense that I won't allow myself to think of it again now—he had been living in Rapallo, Italy, and had organized a series of concerts which attracted wide attention.

Ezra and I had always been worlds apart in musical tastes, and even in *Little Review* days his musical loyalties offered me a target for controversy. Years later, during his imprisonment, I refused to go to the concerts he urged me to hear (so that I could report to him what he himself wasn't free to hear). "My report would be no good to you," I wrote him. "I can't sit through such programs, they represent all that I dislike musically." I should have explained further that if obliged to listen to such programs I would become a person who hath no music in her soul.

Ezra's Rapallo concerts presented the kind of music loved by all intellectuals—those frozen classics of the uninspired world. And, in presenting them, it is said that he preferred to use local Rapallo talent instead of professional performers, as if he feared the latters' virtuosity would betray the music's "intrinsic worth." This preference—for reasons which irritate me—is supposed to preserve "purity."

My preference is the virtuoso and his infinite nuances. To sit through a concert with inferior violinists and pianists scraping through performances of Haydn, Scarlatti, Clementi, Hindemith, Bartók, Britten . . . no, no, preserve me from this undynamic sphere. It is well represented by the Sunday afternoon concerts given in Paris which draw the greatest applause for the interpreters' greatest inadequacies in structure, time, tempo and tone.

My love of virtuosity lies outside virtuosity itself, and my mental response to its transcendence isn't what interests me. One must be a virtuoso to be able to do what one conceives, but it's what is conceived that matters, and that mustn't be mangled. Virtuosity is only "a passing presence" in beautiful playing. The great pianist, to me, is the one whose virtuosity allows him to achieve "the small perfect thing" which distinguishes between what is merely praiseworthy and what is overwhelming.

These masteries and distinctions mark the disques I search for, lie in wait for, love love love, and play happily ever after. I am a musical dilettante in the Proustian sense (with the Saint-Saens [?] "little phrase"), but, I hope, unrelated to those "celibates of art," those people he described as

> more wrought up over works of art than the real artists . . . their emotional state is therefore diffused in outward expression, puts heat into their remarks and blood into their faces . . . This unexpected passion exuberates even into their calmest conversation and leads them to indulge in grand gestures, facial distortions and noddings of the head when they talk of art . . . The music lover's face assumes an anxious expression, as if he were saying to himself, "Why, I see sparks, I smell something burning; there must be a fire somewhere."

Even in the music about which intellectuals and I agree, we never agree about the same movements and moments. If anyone wants to play Vivaldi to me, he must play the section of *The Four Seasons* I love—the end of "Winter." But the moderns prefer the "vigour" of the opening movement, and all the rest that is the most trumpeting. How much of such vigour can you stand? And does it belong to the music you need for your life's extra life?

Oh, I know how well the intellectual can defend his position, I know all his arguments, know them so well that I even respect them; I can present them for him and they sound better than my own. But I can never accept them. The passion for perfection in performance which I so crave exists for the intellectual only in relation to literature. In music, almost any performance will do if the music performed is to his taste. This is where the arguments become confused.

Taste. Perfection. Have such terms any meaning in Art? What would you mean if you said that a poet, a painter, a composer must be "perfect" to qualify as a great artist? A senseless phrase, but the term makes sense in relation to virtuosity. The artist-interpreter must be "perfect" in the sense that he can cast a spell. If he doesn't he remains merely an interpreter, creating nothing. He may even create "imperfectly," as Mary Garden sometimes did when she couldn't manage her high notes. But the fact that she could sing "Annie Laurie" as she did . . . that is the essential perfection, that is the secret and the distinction. And it is this perfection that the intellectual can dispense with, that he even fails to hear.

I like to irritate scholars by quoting Diderot: "Je voudrais savoir où est l'école où l'on apprend à *sentir?*" (Where is the school in which one can learn to *feel?*) Where did Georgette *learn* the charm in which she enveloped her "Invitation au Voyage?" Where did Mary Garden *learn* the pathos of her "Annie Laurie"? Not from her life, apparently. By her own confession she seems never to have experienced heartbreak love ("I'd lay me down and die"), or romantic love (the-world-well-lost). When she talked of love she always spoke of her mother.

But no one has expressed the desolation of Gretchaninoff's "La Steppe" or the sorrow of "Afton Water" as she has. Learn to feel? All you have to do to feel is to be able to feel.

The difference between noncreative life and the aesthetic life interests me more than other subject-matters. I like to argue it out with myself (once again) like this:

The source of the life of emotions (as we kept trying to prove in the *Little Review*) may be that certain people, inspirationally deprived, need to find some salvation from emotional insufficience.

"Not at all," says my opponent. "You destroy your own argument. Everyone feels deprivation. It's merely one of the 'emotions of life'."

Yes, I answer, it usually is *only* that: you *feel* your suffering and that's all you do. But if you want to you can become conscious of it, and consciousness raises your feelings to the status of emotions. Consciousness is the state which gives you a higher human position. Some peoples' nature compels them to transcend their feelings. They become expressive, they become artists—they write *Wuthering Heights,* they compose "Tristan."

Everyone knows the intellectual's reaction to "Tristan." He is not only indifferent, he is often disgusted. It is easy to deride Wagner's sometimes thick emotions, as Rupert Brooke did. On the other hand, if that is all you feel about "Tristan," if your heart hasn't succumbed to the love potion, you are excluded forever from being carried beyond yourself by love, or by that transmutation which transforms feelings into emotions.

Now for a little serious triviality.

Beauty. I've never found, any more than anyone else has, a satisfying definition of beauty. The most inept is that it exists in the eye of the beholder. *What* beholder?

"Truth is beauty, beauty truth" . . . a valid definition? Not at all. Surely both can be decently defined, and the proper "beholder" properly indicated. I've much to say—preferably in words of one syllable.

One can discuss beauty, conclusively, in terms you would use to define "chic." Isak Dinesen writes of "that particular form of intelligence which we call chic."

There are people who profess to despise chic in clothes, but everyone recognizes its presence. Some people know how to dress, others don't. Those who dress badly have no use for chic, they say, but even in their disdain they react to it as to a revolver shot; they stop dead before it, their derision unspoken.

It's different with beauty. Everyone recognizes the beauty of a classically perfect face, but to many people more subtle beauty is invisible. Some say that Garbo is not beautiful, was not beautiful, and is now ugly. The truth is that she was the most beautiful; hers was the face of the century. Something in that face established the legend of beauty, and this legend will never be destroyed—for those who *know*. (Who are they? You know.)

I've been searching for a definition of beauty during the last month, but without success. The only dictionary I have here (Webster's New World) defines it as "that which gives the highest degree of pleasure to the senses or to the mind and suggests that the object of delight approximates to one's conception of the ideal." Dear, dear. Or as "the quality attributed to whatever pleases or satisfies in certain ways, as by line, colour, form, texture, proportion, rhythmic motion," etc. Difficult to imagine anything funnier or more fatuous than "in certain ways."

Beauty, like chic, has the effect of a revolver shot, but unlike chic it sometimes produces its effect only upon the trained eye. Thus Orage's "de gustibus non est disputandum" applies to the situation: the effect produced by chic, being universal, is the proof that "it is so"; the effect produced by beauty is not universal, it can be disputed and thus there is no cessation of debate. It is as elusive as finding a definition of art. "Exagération à propos" may be acceptable as a definition of art, but not of beauty. Berenson could do no better than to define both art and beauty as "life-enchanting." Such talk is sympathetic, one knows what he means, but the statement has no quality of definition.

Suppose that you are discussing beauty in terms of life— what is beautiful in human behaviour? You can say that tact is a beautiful quality because it is based on kindness; and you can also say that good manners are beautiful because they too are based on kindness. Then you can confuse the issue by remembering certain unkind people who have beautiful manners. So there's nothing more to say except that good manners are always at least *physically* beautiful.

I give up, I can't produce a definition. The United Nations, I'm told, hasn't yet found a definition of aggression. This should be child's play. A burglar is an aggressor, or a guest whom you haven't *urged* to come; even a person given to *commenting* can be a most unwelcome aggressor; or—more painful—a person who wants to be your friend even though you don't want him to, since he lacks what is called perception.

Perhaps beauty is a quality—in people, animals, objects— discernible only to those endowed with aesthetic perception. And aesthetic perception is . . .

As to perception, examine two photographs of the same person. Both may be likenesses, therefore both are true; both resemble the subject at different moments, but one may have been taken at a fortunate moment, with expert lighting, and the other at a bad moment, with calculatedly abominable light-

ing—like some of the more ghastly conceptions of Richard Avedon. (The penalty for this crime should not be named.) With
the exception of some ten beautiful photographs (like the Gianni
Agnelli), I have seen none of his that isn't a total desecration
—except, curiously, the one of Janet Flanner. Since Janet isn't
photogenic, he didn't have to destroy her to be happy; she remains, under his demonical eye, as she really is—handsome and
agonized. Who could be more unphotogenic than Eleanor Roose-
velt? But I've seen, of all the horrors to which she was subjected,
one photograph in which she was at her best. This is the kind
of truth that is important, that becomes art; it is the subject's
eternal moment. Avedon, given a chance, could do as much
evil to Garbo as he did to Dinesen, Chanel, and the others;
and imagine what he could do to the supremely photogenic
faces of Anthony Eden, Angus Ogilvy, Peter O'Toole, Alain
Delon, James Dean, even the "too handsome" Mayor Lindsay
(as I now hear him described).

Only the photograph that is beautiful as well as true will
be art. So what is the overwhelming value of truth? There are
too many kinds of truth. The photographer whose beholder's
eye is unseeing is true to the deficiency within him. If he doesn't
know (or is glad to know) that footlights destroy any face, he
produces a monstrosity, but he has produced footlight truth—
a quite unnecessary feat. Modern photographers can reduce
bones to formlessness, and change a face of the most strange,
exquisite and unfathomable beauty into the face of a club-
woman.

I know another photographer of the Avedon type. Once
some friends and I watched him at work on a "study" of a
woman whose good looks lent themselves to various conceptions
of what she "really was." "Shall I emphasize her mondaine
side?" he mused, "or her other aspect which suggests a practical
peasant-like sturdiness?" He opted (a good verb for him) for
the practical aspect, he "made" her into a peasant doing her

89

morning shopping. Well, art is "something made," so he considered his achievement a masterpiece. It was so destructive of any reality into which the subject could have transformed herself that we all struggled and fought with him until we could make him destroy the plates.

I once showed two photographs of a handsome man to someone who disagreed with my ideas of beauty. In one the man looked like a knight and a poet; in the other he looked like a businessman. He was a little of all three, so both photographs were true. But one was beautiful.

Is a poet's face always more beautiful than a businessman's? No. But it should be. Art is "should be."

If you can't hide the sad fact that your face is unlovely, or ugly, and if your photographer can't hide it, then don't be photographed; or don't be seen. You can say that you "want to be alone," you can wear a veil, or you can ask your friends not to look at you; even during a conversation they can look at the sea instead of at you.

"Don't talk so foolishly," says one of my critics. "Other people are photographed at your age without being vain about it. Look at Dinesen."

"Yes, do look at her. She has bones and features. I haven't."

"You are maddening. There's such a thing as spiritual beauty."

"Don't madden *me*. I know all about 'spiritual beauty.' I haven't got it."

But, as in life, when one sees an ugly or insipid face transfigured under deep emotion, so in photography almost any face can be irradiated by the metamorphic influence of art. The trouble today is that photographers prefer disfigurement to adornment. It is now chic to do your worst to people.

Since Art is "should be," it can also be "as if." Beauty "is." As you see, I can talk as metaphysically as Sartre of Dr. Suzuki; but this doesn't help me to define beauty, or the particular form of intelligence which is its province; or explain why only a few people are born with the aesthetic eye.

Painted trees are often more beautiful than real trees. On the other hand, I remember real trees in the *War and Peace* film that were more beautiful than any painted trees I ever saw. Once, at an exhibition, Berenson had been looking for hours at Chinese paintings of trees in snowy landscapes. The light of day was fading in the museum, and when he looked out at trees in the window he mistook them for a painting and exclaimed, "Look, look, these are the finest trees of all."

An Etruscan horse's head is more beautiful than that of any real horse, but a real horse is sometimes grandly beautiful. In that case you have to decide whether the statue or the real horse is the more beautiful. It will always be the statue. Why? Because Art is like that. It can transfigure or transform or transcend all things—except human beings. As a human being, a great painter remains at 70 what he was at 7. It takes something more than Art to change his status-quo life to a more conscious state.

. . . But to continue with *my* status quo:

The look of things . . . this is my ever-present preoccupation. I can't close my eyes to the strange necessity of dwelling on what is good-looking and avoiding what is ugly; or transforming the latter into the former. This necessity exists in all realms, even the most trivial.

For example, the matches I buy in France come in little paquets, one side of which is ugly, the other good-looking. Wherever I am I automatically turn the ugly side face-down so that I won't have to look at it. I do this in my friends' houses as well as in my own, and I laughed the other day when my hostess said, "After you leave I'm not going to turn the matches right-side-up any more." I said, "Even when I put a paquet in the wastebasket I look to make sure that the good-looking side is turned up."

It is the same with poetry.

Consider the *look* of words. Do you like to read ugly words? Don't they make ugly poems? Place two poems side by side and look at them:

"Rehabilitation Center"

In the good suburb, in the bursting season,
their canes awag in the yellow day,
the newly maimed wince back back to danger.

Cave by cave they come to building their hearing
hard as fists against the jangling birds,
the slipslop of car wheels, wall mimicries,

[Etc., etc.]

Under a wide sky let them cry now
to be coddled, misread a tree, black shins
or crack their knees on countermands;
The downgrade is uncertain for us all.

[Etc.]

—Maxine Kumin

Then examine the second poem:

"Imaginary Marriage"

The trees are heavy with dancing lemons.
The young boys sparkle in the shadows.
The blind horizon is searched for omens.
Poppies are picked in the spotted meadows.

The old men polish their antique arrows.
The groom's mother stands in her stiff lace.
The children hop among the sparrows,
and the fountain breaks the drinker's face.

The dead clasp one another, and the dumb
rustle their hopeless sticks; the dog, forgotten
in the yellow courtyard, is sick with the sun.

In her room, the bride's sister has been weeping;
her brother's vest is flowered with wine.
The bride stands in the mirror, scarcely breathing,
looped like a statue with cool columbine.

The groom is in the hall; with a belt of silver
that will not clasp; and a sense of danger
tires him, until he has lost the savor
of himself, and feels himself a stranger.

The match is made under a crown of candles
In the pink cathedral webbed a faint fire.
Down avenues of saints in their stone sandals
an immense desire spreads outward like a stair.

The children are shy now with their drunken fathers.
In the furnace of August the lepers walk
among their pennies; and the carmine feathers
in the cage rustle; and the heart is like chalk.

And the rivers flash with their tinsel minnows,
the stars circle their sapphire clocks.
The lizards rest on the cool hands of the windows,
and the gold moves slowly in the rocks.

—Robert Horan

Horan's beautiful sharp words . . . just to look at them is
enough, quite apart from their meaning. I can't read the other
poem because my eyes refuse to look at the words, they won't
accept such boredom, such nonsense; they dart away as from
an offense.

———

I've just finished reading nineteen volumes of Paul Léautaud's *Journal Littéraire*. It's a rare, original, honest, human

document full of personal information. It's clearly, cleanly, and simply written, and probably no one has ever revealed more truth about himself and his way of life (tragic, hilarious, sensitive, pathetic and often terribly repugnant); but in its thousands of pages I remember no phrase that imposes a new world upon your mind or emotions, leaving you unconscious of everything else.

The absence of the state of art in Léautaud isn't surprising. He disliked art, or kept saying that he did. He hated "the beautiful phrase," "the great phrase"; he liked only a spontaneous outpouring, unworked on afterward—or so he said—and then inconsistently refused to republish *Le Petit Ami* until he had revised it. Not being an artist in the full meaning of the word, his revisions were never luminous; in fact they usually ruined what he had written in the first flow of feeling.

To the end he kept repeating, "I hate art." He didn't know the difference between "fine writing" and art; hating the former, he confused the latter with it. He rejected Proust—"too many words"—as if art were a matter of few or many words. "Art is air, an atmosphere," said Dinesen, but Léautaud wouldn't have known what she meant. He loved Stendhal and loathed Flaubert. I reread Flaubert's *L'Education Sentimentale* in English the other day and found it curiously lacking in trouvailles; so I reread it in French and found the same lack. Whatever its other qualities, I began to wonder why Flaubert's reputation rests on an agonized search for le mot juste. I think his search was for something else, so I appreciate his judgment, his structures, and his style more than his words. I love to reread his letters. One of them—to Louise Colet—is probably the funniest letter ever written; I reread it whenever I need a fou rire. Louise had sent him a poem she had written about her baby daughter. Flaubert, always severe about her poetry, particularly disliked some lines in the poem, "A Ma Fille":

De ton joli corps sous la couverture
Plus souple apparaît le contour charmant;
Tel au Parthénon quelque frise pure
Nous montre une vierge au long vêtement.

He considered the first two lines "obscene." "And then," he went on, "what is the Parthénon doing there, so close to your daughter's blanket?"

Even Stendhal often disappoints me in respect of trouvailles. Searching through the 500 pages of *Le Rouge et le Noir* the other day, I came upon very few. Stendhal almost never took pains in describing his characters: "C'était une jeune fille mince, assez grande, avec un nez aquilin, jolie, svelte, bien faite." No writer today would dream of such inertia—our literary nerves have too long been accustomed to special turns of language, simple new ways, or refreshing old ways of seeing. *Henri Brulard*, which Léautaud considered one of the great books, is to me one of the dullest ever written.

If, like Léautaud, you prefer narrative that relates the facts and nothing but the facts, Stendhal usually does; and this, I suppose, is why Gide said that Stendhal wasn't his nourriture. If you want all that exists beyond facts, you are glad that Racine dealt with emotions like this:

Dans un mois, dans un an, comment souffrirons-nous,
Seigneur, que tant de mers me séparent de vous;
Que le jour recommence et que le jour finisse,
Sans que jamais Titus puisse voir Bérénice . . .

But Léautaud scorned such poetry. "Oh, c'est très joli," he said, "mais tout ça pour dire 'Cher ami, avez-vous pensé qu'on ne peut plus se voir'? Oh non! Vraiment!"

Vraiment, I say, *expression* is everything. In this respect Stendhal's letters are more rewarding to me than his novels. "It is my natural bent to live with two candles and a writing-table." Or:

I was much madder, but also much happier when, without saying a word to anyone, and when I was already a grown man and appending my signature to official documents, I kept on thinking of the passions that I was on the eve of experiencing, feeling, and perhaps inspiring. The details of a handclasp beneath tall trees at night caused me to indulge in day-dreams for hours on end.

Ah, those tall trees at night . . . *Expression.*

Some critic once said that Stendhal could make a sentence turn on a dime. I'm not sure that I know exactly what he meant, but I've found an example that seems to "turn" perfectly . . . one of Max Beerbohm's incomparable little sentences, in a description of his old school at Charterhouse: "My delight at having been there was (don't you know) far greater than had been my delight in being there."

Unless for expression, why read a book twice? I can't imagine reading *Le Rouge et le Noir* or *La Chartreuse* twice. But I can read Proust over and over, always skipping certain too long passages of "cultural" research, because I read for the ambiance that surrounds the writer's being. Who could resist reading twice, or more, a book which begins "Longtemps je suis couché de bonne heure"?

I couldn't read Léautaud's *Journal* twice. Gide's? Yes. Because, as Léautaud himself admitted, "Gide's *Journal* has more interior life in it than mine has."

Léon Blum called *Le Petit Ami* a little book full of literature. It is just that. But no claim to literature has ever revealed less of the *state* of art. Léautaud was as unconcerned with the beauty I've been talking about as a concierge would be.

———

I sometimes plan to compose an anthology which would include only those gems of great poetry and prose which I have greatly loved and want to read over and over. I would omit certain mighty classics. For instance, Homer.

Can I justify such an omission? I think so.

I'm never tempted to reread the *Iliad* or the *Odyssey,* in spite of the wine-dark sea and the face that launched the ships. I never forget that these epic stories fall within the Nine Eternal Moods—Love, Hate, Fury, Pity, Terror, Despair, Remorse, Awe (I always forget the ninth). I know their grandeur, but it's a grandeur I can dispense with. I don't want to read about wars any more than I want to fight in a war. There's no compulsion in me to identify with the "sad and savage story of men" and their unnecessary fate in war. Let Homer make "the roar of war ring loudly in our ears with a furious grandeur . . ." I don't want to hear this roar. I am outside such goings-on.

Accuse me if you like of an unfailing predilection for the minor in Art—I am unperturbed; and in any case I would rather be scorned by critics for rejoicing in Wordsworth's daffodils than praised for intoning the sonorities of Homer's battles. I'm quite unashamed to admit that I'm interested only in battles of ideas.

How can anyone be *interested* in war?—that glorious pursuit of annihilation with its ceremonious bellowings and trumpetings over the mangling of human bones and muscles and organs and eyes, its inconceivable agonies which could have been prevented by a few well-chosen, reasonable words. How, why, did this unnecessary business begin? Why does anyone want to read about it—this redundant human madness which men accept as inevitable? If you're involved in it, you die; if you read about it, you can't sleep. Therefore my anthology will ignore it.

My real justification for omitting Homer goes deeper. After all, did these ancient stories convey the "conscious" knowledge of antiquity? From what I have heard, they did not. The lessons they taught should have been learned long since. New tragic myths will be created. "Fare forward, voyager" will refer to a possible new fate for man . . . not concerned with his explorations in space, but with those within himself.

97

Solita reproaches me periodically, "Why won't you study?"

"Because I don't want to know more than I already know."

"You don't want to know more . . . !" She is too repelled to go on.

"Of course not. Why should I? I only like to know what I find out for myself, from myself."

She wants to leave the room, but I continue. "Anything I learn by studying I forget. What I learn from myself I never forget." If given a chance to go on (almost never), I say that I don't in the least mind being illiterate, I'm satisfied with being educated.

"You think you are educated?"

"Certainly. That is, I'm a person 'who can entertain a new idea, entertain another person, and entertain herself.' I am therefore very educated." To which Solita says that I'm only being wily.

But there's no reason to be wily about so serious a subject as the difference between knowledge and understanding. No reason to be over-serious either. You can win the argument without effort.

My trivia reside less in my subject-matter than in the unintellectual way I like to talk about it. This is dangerous, since critics are disconcerted by simple discourse—they think it springs from mindlessness.

When critics are good they awe me by their insight, by their gift of interpreting the writer as he hopes, but rarely expects, to be understood. When they are bad—and the most erudite are the worst—they appall me by their inability to understand anything at all. They are the people who don't understand what they know.

Why should I want to know more than I understand?

A musical example: Bach's Chorale, "I Call upon Thee, Jesus." "What is the final chord resolution?" someone asks me, assuming that I know more about it than he does. But I don't. Never having studied harmony, I have no idea whether this chorale ends on a dominant or a tonic chord. I never think of needing to know such things. What would I gain in emotion (in ambition, yes) by being able to say that Bach had ended his chorale on such or such a chord? I *hear* what he did, I don't need to *know* anything about it. This divine music is the music of consolation. As you listen to that final chord your heart will become still for a moment, freed of grief.

Oh, the absurdities of musicologists! They write articles to help the unmusical understand music. There's nothing to understand, only to marvel at. Music is a miracle. Since a miracle has been defined as "the laws of one cosmos operating in another," you will have to have had some special experience of life if you're going to "understand" anything. The explanations of pedants can tell you what is going on in music, but they can't make you understand it, they can't even make you hear it. Understanding is "the experience of overwhelming emotions" (Ezra?); or, in Gurdjieff's words, "Understanding is arrived at by personal-experiences-personally-experienced"; and knowledge (in Orage's beautiful translation of the Gurdjieff text) "is only a passing presence in it."

I once heard a pianist say of another pianist, "He's not a musician OR a pianist, but he's an artist." He was saying, I trust, that what the artist knows cannot be taught; but he added so much about musicianship that I couldn't be sure what he really meant.

Good musicianship has only a little to do with being an

artist. Anyone can become a good musician if he wants to, and of course he should want to. One can even *become* a composer, but who wants to? Unless you're a born composer you'll never be an authentic one. If you're a born one, you learn your mé-tier afterward—just as a born writer, painter, pianist, singer does. You learn—with great or little effort—all that can be learned; but your gift came from heaven and consists of all that cannot be taught. I know a person who plays by ear, who can replay any melodic theme once she has heard it; who can name (without thinking) every note in the scale on which a melody is based, who can improvise, and compose (but only in the keys of C and G). If you ask her how she knows all this, does all this, she can't explain, and she can no longer do it.

I get so tired of talk about knowledge that even today I still feel a need to assert myself when people tell me that I don't know what I'm talking about. Someone asked a friend of mine not long ago, "Is Margaret's talk as crazy as her writing?"

When I was young—in the year when we moved the *Little Review* from Chicago to New York—it hadn't occurred to me that anyone who doesn't know all that cannot be taught would ever aspire to be a music critic. At our first soirée in New York there was a discussion about music, since one of the eminent New York music critics was present. Not knowing who he was, and finding his conversation highly stupid, I cried out, to everyone's consternation, "But don't you know *anything* about music?"

When I was still younger, in the Chicago days before I had started the *Little Review*, I was invited to tea by the Little Room Club—a group of Chicago artists and notables who met in Lorado Taft's studio in the Fine Arts Building. The pianist Fannie Bloomfield Zeisler was then a great celebrity, and I was thrilled to find myself sitting beside her. She told me how much she regretted not being able to enjoy concerts the way other people did. "I sit in the audience listening to someone playing the piano beautifully, but because I *know* too much about what is happening I *feel* nothing at all."

I have always suspected that too much knowledge is a dangerous thing. It is a boon to people who don't have deep feelings; their pleasure comes from what they know about things, and their pride from showing off what they know. But this only emphasizes the difference between the artist and the scholar. There are predominantly "emotional-center" people and predominantly "mental-center" people, and I thought these distinctions were too well known to need new discussion.

Emotional-center people say, with truth, "I don't quite know what it *means*, but I feel that I understand it." Mental-center people are often like the man to whom Gurdjieff said, "You do not understand what you read or what you write. You do not even understand what the word 'understand' means."

The intellectual critic tells you how Bach composed his music, and thus teaches you to love Bach. There's nothing more false than the idea that you can learn to love music because someone explains how it was written ("If you study it you'll soon come to love it.") You can cultivate a taste for caviar, and you can cultivate a *taste* for music; but you can't cultivate a *love* of music. You must love it from your beginning, before you knew anything about it.

Professional critics write about "the orderly ingenuity shown in Bach's 'Goldberg Variations.'" What is the interest in his having produced three or thirty orderly, ingenious variations on a single theme? The point is: do you (as a touchstone) love the theme, do you want to listen to it all your life, knowing instinctively that it belongs to the indefinable world of Art?

I instantly loved the first Debussy I heard (how many years ago?). Its difference from the music we knew raised no barrier. The first Hindemith I heard left me irritated, weary, vastly bored—and still does. You may dislike a person at first, then grow to like him later. But this experience has never happened to me in music.

Perhaps I tell a pianist friend that I don't like his conception of a certain Chopin Etude—"I think you break up the structure, and that bothers me." (Shouldn't have told him, should have remembered that he becomes personal in discussion.)

Infuriated, he speaks loudly. "My structure is perfect! Everyone tells me so: 'You're wonderful, don't you ever miss a note?' I answer that I have too much respect for structure to miss notes!"

I say, "Missing notes has nothing to do with structure. I don't mind how many notes Horowitz misses. If a building is made of bricks, and a few fall out, that leaves a few holes in the surface of the building but doesn't destroy its structure, its design, its architecture."

Still angry. "It's extraordinary! You always think you're right about everything."

"No, I don't. I think I'm right *for myself*. What's more, I can't see why my criticism bothers you. I'm not a musician, I *know* almost nothing about music and nothing at all about harmony."

"You must be neurotic. You're full of manias."

"Exactly. My life has been based on those manias and nothing is going to change them. Don't give them a thought."

Mind to mind, I have a great bond with my nephew, Fritz Peters,* a brilliant example of the mental-emotional type. He has told me about his experience with an excellent but academic piano teacher:

"At the time when I was studying harmony with her she said, 'Margaret never understood that a knowledge of harmony

---

* Author of *Boyhood with Gurdjieff*, etc. (London: Gollancz, Ltd.)

would make music much more exciting to her.' [To be more excited is just what I don't need, as Fritz knew.] I refrained from arguing at the time (perhaps wisely?), but I remember thinking that I was unable to explain a difference to her: the study of harmony did fascinate my *mind;* when I was able to say to myself that Chopin achieved such and such an effect by using a dominant-seventh chord, it is true that I was pleased. What my teacher couldn't understand was that I was pleased with my newly acquired ability (i.e., proud of myself), but that the music remained what it was—then. Now, the intrusion of my mind when it insists on recognizing a particular chord only serves to interrupt and temporarily destroy the effect of the music. Music as architecture (chords as bricks) is interesting only to the extent that I am suddenly able to identify the fact that a house is built of cement—but to recognize a brick (or a chord) is, in the long run, deadening. Analysis of music is a fascinating occupation to the intellectual mind—the mind that must *know how.* It is a self-limiting occupation that usually takes the place of emotional response—in fact, tends to prevent emotional response or enjoyment."

Intellectuals are too sentimental for me.

Of course I know a number of likeable, honourable, unpretentious, interesting, and brilliant intellectuals, but there are others I don't care to know. What I most redoubt about these others is not their sterility and pomposity, their fatuity and posturing, their unawareness and superiority, their snobbery and gullibility—I am equipped to deal with such excesses. It's their sentimentality that astonishes and outwits me. As soon as I became aware of this unexpected trait in their natures we became strangers.

Naturally, I began by being (or considering myself to be) an intellectual. But I finished by realizing that this would never do. Even at first such a position made me a little nervous, as if something, something underneath, wasn't quite right. I began to be embarrassed by those people with inferiority complexes who said humbly, "I'm not an intellectual," as if ashamed of not belonging to a superior race. Intellectuals were so revered that artists often felt weak and childish in their presence, and I remember Jane's advice to a creative young pianist who was too easily distraught by any intellectual's disdain. "Take a stand," she said, "develop a repartee to protect yourself. Don't be weakly strong. Be strongly weak."

How true! If you can do that, you'll become a tyrant and everyone will respect you.

My own stand was this: "It's curious that intellectuals know all the things I don't know, and that I know all the things they don't know."

My first disillusionment with my intellectual friends was caused by their horrid way of "talking down" to people. In their critical talk or writing I was always coming upon some unconscious exposure of superiority, some indecent condescension, in the maddening schoolmaster tone: "Shall I explain it to you?" Why that pompous "to you," I wondered; why didn't he say, "Shall we try to explain it"—as if for his own benefit as much as yours.

And then their particular brand of sentimentality began to puzzle me. They managed to inject into their literary criticism ideas, meanings, symbols, which I was sure the authors hadn't intended to convey—the sentimentality of the false note . . . harrowing. I listened to critics overflowing with exaggerated sentiments in a way artists never overflow; they would be ashamed to. This débordement is embarrassing. To what audience is it addressed? It was like the embarrassment we felt in the *Ulysses* trial when we were accused of being a danger to the minds of young girls. Jane's mournful comment was: "If there's anything I really fear it is the mind of the young girl."

I began to distrust most of my intellectual friends in all ways—in their attitudes, their judgments (so wavering), the inexactitudes of their weights and measures, the irresponsibility and unreality of their opinions and their positions. They seemed to sidle into a position toward life, never to have a secure foothold; and the more vociferously they aired their opinions, the more blustering and brilliant they became, the more I felt their insecurity. (The difference between us was that I was blustering but not brilliant.)

The worst was to come, and it separated us forever. I couldn't get used to their non-presence in situations where participation was imperative, and their extravagant participation in situations where silence—and silence only—would have been a sign of intelligence or emotion. Have you ever turned toward an intellectual in a time of authentic anguish and encountered his light appraisal, or evasion, of your grief? Or turned to him in a situation of light import only to be met with a heavy,

105

superfluous solemnity? If there is anything in human behaviour that *I* fear, it is this disorder.

My impressions of the *unreal* were never so strong as when I found myself in a group of pseudo-intellectual thinkers, talkers, writers. I began to ask myself, "How can glittering brains be so far from suspecting the potentialities of the MIND?" And I regaled myself with the story of Ella Fitzgerald's astute evaluation of herself: "I'm not a musician. I'm more of a singer, I guess." "Ah," I said, "I'm not an intellectual. I'm more of a mind than a brain, I guess."

At last I gave up trying to communicate with my brainy colleagues. My final condemnation was: they are intellectual, but not intelligent. I couldn't stop counting the number of ways in which we were separated in our considerations of all things. I remember a conversation with a man whose writing I had already admired, but who said to me one day, at a distressing cocktail party, "I could have, *should* have perhaps, taken on a Gurdjieff group, but I'm afraid it would have bored me too much." This from a man in whom Gurdjieff had been trying (in vain) to arouse some understanding of his teaching.

One thing became clear, and of course it came from Gurdjieff. A pure intellectual is a one-centered being (mental center); an artist is a combination of two centers (mental-emotional). One might make an Einsteinian formula:

$E + M = A$. (Emotion plus mind = Art)

The academic mind shouldn't attempt to write biographies of artists. But then who should? Only artists. An artist can interpret another artist, but a scholar doesn't know what goes on in an artist's mind.

At this moment a pleasant and conscientious young scholar is writing a history of the *Little Review,* and has shown me his manuscript. I applauded his untiring research, but I was discouraged by many of his interpretations of "what happened." No fault of his, of course; how could he have differentiated between legend and truth except by becoming *me*?

I told him, first, that there was no need for a history of the magazine; I had already put into a *Little Review Anthology* what I considered its history. Second, I said that the "facts" contributed by most witnesses of our delightful and incredible story (history) were often as fantastically distorted as Lawrence Langner's report of an afternoon he spent with us in our camp on the beach (details later) during one of those intervals when we had no other place to live. Emma Goldman came out to see us, and Lawrence's anecdote presents her as a disagreeable woman who was complaining about the discomforts of beach life—the heat, the mosquitos, the sand . . . The truth was the opposite: she was playing a role, making a charming little drama out of the discomforts, and we were all appreciating it except Lawrence, who was a person without the seeing eye—the kind who makes a farce of history or biography because he can't feel his way into the lives of the people he is writing about.

My historian's reaction to the corrections I made in his manuscript was: "Some of your suggestions are in the realm of personal opinion and, while I believe in no one's opinions more completely than yours, I think we *do* have a few honest disagreements."

"Well, we mustn't have," I said. "It's better not to enter into a contest with me because I shall defeat you. It's entirely a matter of personal opinion, and it's my opinions that made the *Little Review* what it was. So it will do no good for you to present yours."

This very nice antagonist represents one of the three classes of critics who make history dangerous ground to tread on: 1) the writer limited in human-nature experience; 2) the intellectual trying to create out of an imagined reality; 3) the scholar wandering, lost, in the valid, but alien dimensions of his subject's personal information.

A propos of all these ramblings, there is a Simon & Schuster man who writes in defense of publishers: "It's awfully hard for a real writer to remain undiscovered, unless he is trying to remain that way. Editors *want* to discover real talent, and live in the hope of doing so every day."

What foolish words! What kind of man is speaking? What kind of editors does he think are judging real talent? What makes him think they are competent? To what note in the scale of human hierarchies do they belong? What has been the level of their life experience? Why *hope* to discover unless you know what you should hope for?

Suppose I am forced to stand trial by jury. Who will be chosen as my peers? Where will they be found? How many of them are there? Will they be like the three judges who condemned, and fined, and fingerprinted me for publishing *Ulysses* in the *Little Review*?

At that trial (during which two of the judges fell asleep, and the third—a Norwegian—said afterward that had he known that Jane was a Norwegian he would have changed the verdict), we might possibly have found twelve jurors who could understand Joyce (though I'm not sure of it). They would have been my peers, since I too could understand him. And then there would have been no trial. We would all have pronounced *Ulysses* a masterpiece, and I wouldn't have been a criminal.

It would be even better to be judged by one's superiors than by one's peers. A superior man is one who knows what's what, a man who understands all things. In a trial before his superiors, *any* criminal would stand a chance of justice. From my experience with editors and publishers, the S&S man wouldn't have been among the superiors.

108

I have a story which should subdue him:

Georgette wrote a book of "Souvenirs" for which Cocteau did a Preface. The French critics hailed it: "A book so tragic, so moving, constitutes an extremely rare event. Nothing so beautiful, so strong, has appeared in many years" (Pierre Descaves); "A book Stendhal would have loved, for all that it contains of the rare and the true"; "Genius overflows in this book —literary and psychological genius"; "A lyric poet—a feminine mind perhaps the most interesting of our time"; "A genre without precedence in the history of letters"; "Georgette Leblanc can introduce all the mystery of human destiny in a gesture, in a word"; "A vast tragic novel of the heart and the brain."

Every first-grade publishing house in America refused it. All called it a "beautiful document, beautifully written," but since it hadn't "the slightest chance of commercial success," and since the S&S man didn't want to "discover its talent," it has remained unpublished in America.

What other reason could be given for its rejection? For one, Georgette and Maeterlinck were no longer in the public eye. For another, it wasn't a book of talent, it was a work of genius.

I'm not vindictive about these editors who don't understand books of genius. I'm shocked by them—outraged, repulsed, and amused. They have never lived in my world, nor I in theirs, and we don't want to hear about each other's.

Solita expressed better than anyone else this abyss between two worlds, in a letter she wrote to calm my furious frustration:

Georgette's book is bound *not* to be a success with the public. It is a record of her unique valor and tragedy. It is special for people who react to a great, illumined nature of inner struggles, all of which are individual (personal) to her. Now (and this is "why," as you're about to ask indignantly) other such rich natures have succeeded with the public, given same qualities, characteristics, above enumerated for Georgette. But they (other writers) were concerned with War and Peace struggles,

Social Injustice (Tolstoy), political waverings (Sheean, *Personal History*), religion (as such), so that their strivings were identified in the reader as his own poor little speculations or pangs of conscience. Somehow Georgette's strivings do not make the reader (general, not like us) feel "This is just like me, what I've always felt or thought consciously or unconsciously." She is too remote (yet she wasn't at all in life) on paper, too abstract for the public; you can deny, but impression on reader remains. Only people like us will understand and weep for her aloneness in her real life, as I do every time I read her ms. Yes, I know that you know what is great, near-great, or good. And I believe I do too. But you do not know, as I do, that the law you believe in— that everyone really recognizes a great work—does not operate much of the time, and, in Georgette's case, less than anyone else's. I don't know why. No one would be more happy to say with shining face that the public would agree with me. I just cannot say it. I think, and can't help it, that the public will ignore everything in the book that we treasure, and in exact proportion to how much we feel, so will it (they) be unresponsive. Another thought: Georgette does not "put over" on paper to people what they do not already know (feel); to people who *do* know (feel), she puts over doubly. I think this is the answer— one aspect anyway.

Through the book I absorb something of Georgette, and never stop learning from the delicate avocations she puts forth like little tendrils for special needs. Though dead, she remains a living source of "adorability"—plus her unworldly knowledge—and she has enriched my life, not only once again, but more than ever, both for pain and understanding.

I agree with this penetrating evaluation except for one statement: I believe there *is* a public for certain great books which publishers reject. I've never shown Georgette's manuscript (in our two-volume English translation) to any American representative of the *aspiring general public* without receiving from him a reaction as intense as that of the French critics. It is the S&S man and his ilk (hideous, perfect label) who lack this perceptive response. And then of course—like any other "great person"—Georgette was so different from "people" that they couldn't say, "This is just like us."

One can't quarrel with publishers. They are in business to make money, and it would be foolish to be in business for any other reason. But great orchestras don't make money, and grand opera doesn't make money, and the people who pay their deficits do it because orchestras and operas exist not for business but for Art. So I often wonder why some publisher doesn't announce to the world, "I shall publish only books which are ART. Help!!" This is what the *Little Review* did, and a valiant new publisher would be as surprised as we were at the response —aesthetic and financial—he would receive. We kept alive for fifteen years on this shaky basis. We never had more than a few dollars at a time, but during all those years no one who was asked to help refused, except one millionaire—multimillionaire, I believe—who promised to put us on our feet with a contribution of $4,000. But after I had had tea with him and he had clarified his position to me: "A great singer I know wanted pearls, but you, you only want the *Little Review.* . . ." Well, I refused his next invitation to tea and he refused the $4,000.

———

Exciting *Little Review* days! Dwight Macdonald described them well in the *New Yorker:* "One had the impression that the *Little Review* was a lot of fun to write for, to read, to edit . . . its sense of life, of discovery, of enjoyment—its sense of conversation, which means being able to disagree and still continue the discussion; fights—hot and impolite; insult and jeering, to bring a definite and creative hardness to the pulp of art in America."

I have still another story about those eager editors so un-eager toward the art of literature:

A few years after the publication and bestseller success of Dorothy's *Caruso* book, she wrote another—the story of her after-Caruso life. Simon & Schuster refused it. Even after the first book's commercial success they didn't want to go on. Why? The second book was better than the first one. It had the quality of a narrative poem, and I could quote a hundred passages brimming with trouvailles which prove its poetic content and form. Do I blame S&S for their rejection? No. I simply want to prevent that man from babbling further about editors' infal-lible recognition of talent.

Since the book was presented in the language of images, with the mind in control but its processes hidden, a *New Yorker* critic called it "mindless." I wondered if that critic had never read Proust: "An artist has no need to express his mind directly in order to express the quality of that mind." Or Orage: "Thought is not only not art, but the aim of art is to conceal thought."

In other words, our additional formula for the *Little Review* credo:

INTELLECTUALS DO NOT HAVE
AESTHETIC EXPERIENCES.

To critics who like to argue with me I always say, "Better not. I always win."

Example. Poulenc's Intermezzo in A Flat—that most ex-quisite little trifle, with an irresistible little theme which you can't forget.

One of my critics said, "It's too bad you haven't studied harmony. You would realize that your pleasure in this Intermezzo is produced by the cleverness with which Poulenc builds up to the repetition of his original 'little phrase.'"

Ah, the mental gymnastics of the ordinary male mind! I said, "You're laughable. My pleasure came first, before I could have any idea of how Poulenc was going to develop his theme. How could I (or you) realize it in advance? Can you theorize about something before it happens? You are captivated before you know what is going to develop harmonically. On a first hearing you can only listen and say 'What a seductive theme! I hope he repeats it often enough.' On a second hearing you hear that he has repeated it four times. Do you need to know harmony to hear that?"

I can easily win most arguments, but I remember twice when I lost. The first time—in *Little Review* days—was when I said in exasperation, "Give me ecstasy or give me death." And Jane said, "Why limit me to ecstasy?"

The other time was when I went to a Consulate to extract a favour from a U.S. government official for a French singer who was having a hard time with American red-tape:

The consul said, "I can grant no special favours."

"Why not?"

"Because if I do it for one I must do it for everyone."

"Why?"

"You know why, madam."

"No, I don't. Tell me why, please."

"Because everyone is entitled to equal treatment."

"Who is everyone?"

"You know very well, madam, that all people . . ."

"There is no 'everyone.'"

"You are talking nonsense. Everyone is created free and equal."

"Is everyone created a Sarah Bernhardt?"

"No, but . . ."

"Will you ever find another Sarah Bernhardt?"

"I don't know whether I will or not."

"Well, you won't. So you have no problem."

"Madam, you are beginning to exasperate me."

"I'm the exasperated one. Are any two thumbprints alike?"

"No. What has that to do with it?"

"One man's prints may be more refined than another's?"

"I wouldn't know. I have more important things to think about."

"You're not thinking. All thumbprints are not equal, as all things and all people are not equal."

"Thumbprints have nothing to do with the matter at hand."

"I should like to know why not. Some can put you in jail, others . . ."

"Madam, I wouldn't grant you a favour for anyone after this conversation."

"You'll grant that all pianists don't play alike?"

"Yes, but . . ."

"That one may play better than another, and therefore be treated differently?"

"I have nothing to do with pianists. You're not asking a favour for a pianist. You're asking me to make an exception for a singer."

"We've gone into that. Unless you can prove that everyone is a Bernhardt . . ."

"Madam, I will bid you good day."

Someone asks me, "Why don't you write a book yourself that is Art, since you're so enamoured of it and so scornful of writers who don't satisfy you?"

Surely you know why. Because I'm not a writer. I have no relation to words, only to ideas and emotions. I do the best I can to find words for them, but I have to work hard—I have no natural gift. I think I've never met any intelligent person who has such difficulty expressing herself in easy, fluent words as I have. I used to talk breathlessly, which made it easier. Now I've lost even that advantage.

I have always been entranced with, touched and mystified by, the special literature of born writers. All their felicities excite my mind in proportion to my own lack of them. I have a passion also for the craft of rewriting which lesser talents impose upon themselves in order to achieve naturalness. For myself, perhaps at the tenth rewrite something that sounds natural arrives, but it is only in somnolent dreaming or in sleepless night-thinking that it is real.

Solita often helps me with her kind and brutal editing genius. "No, it will *not* do. Weak all over, bland, dull. You must please your readers, not yourself, since you don't seem able to do both at the same time."

Functioning as an appreciator, I am grateful that five of my great friends have been born writers. None of them had planned to be, and three of them began to write without having any knowledge of a métier. The fourth trained herself to become a writer because she needed a newspaper job. She had had no conventional schooling, but had the tenacity to learn four languages (by herself) and the determination to learn them properly. She developed a prose style, and when I read a sentence of hers beginning "Was it music or water?", I cried "A poem! You must finish it." She did, and produced a little volume of poetry entitled *Statue in a Field*, which revealed a gift of using words with bull's-eye precision, and authentic sorrow; simple usual words used in unusual ways.

My fifth friend became a writer by inheritance, by listening to her mother's beautiful spoken prose.

The first three of these friends approached the writing of good prose with the native endowment of poets, and their equipment consisted further of the first great requisites: all three had experienced real heartbreak when young, and again —tragically—later on. All three had known how to face the world again. They had acquired this stature before I knew them, but none of them ever treated my darling-of-the-gods situation as inferior to their own earned position. It was their attitude that allowed me to understand their summits, their richer emotions, the experience of their minds, their unique personal information. They taught me (by example) one of the first lessons of life —how to distinguish between people who are "real" and those who are not. These natural writers are *extreme* people; they are open to, and respond to, all essential impressions. They are real.

From what I have observed, they all create in the same way—*seemingly* without effort, without thought, almost without reflection, as if the knowledge of what they were saying had existed in them from the beginning. They seem not to think, but to *see;* and their thoughts are pictures. When I begin to write I don't see anything at all, I *think* something. No image ever occurs to me. I think, I express the thought, realize that I've not expressed it clearly or with any trace of charm or per-suasion. I think again, edit, reformulate, and all this takes a great deal of time. With born writers all appears to be spon-taneous, instantaneous; they have drawn upon what was waiting in them to make its appearance, like the little boy who said that in making a drawing he simply traced over the lines he already saw drawn on the paper.

(I remember, suddenly, that I did once find an image. It came to me like one of those night thoughts just before troubled sleep, like this: "My head is a forest. I see a tiny figure stumbling through it, trying to find a way out, a path leading to somewhere. The whole top of my head vibrates with the pain of these steps, they press down upon my eyes. I can't see for the pain. I am trying to cut a jungle path through a mind too dense to yield. I must find a way to stop the pain . . . Why did I ever think I could become a writer?")

Georgette described the phenomenon of imagery like this:

A sorrow goes out from me, returns, ascends, descends, only to descend and ascend again and again. I can do nothing about it; if I try to, all is lost. It depends on a vision. I *see* a grief like an image traced by my nerves. It becomes more clear, more precise, it takes on a form, and then falls from me. The story of a fruit tree.

Jane's way of seeing was this:

My heart is an idiot. I write my name and way and pin it on him . . . if we should become separated. With my hands I take my brain and slowly uncrumple it . . . surprising how big it is smoothed out like melted silk. I will crumple it up again firmly and put it back after I have left it this way for a long time shining and clean. The years breed pain when one is accomplice with an idiot.

———————

The craft of my writer friends was made easier by the fact that three of them were amateur painters. No one writes so easily, so vitally, as a painter. For instance: "He had a lively irritated walk, as if he were kicking a stone out of his way." (Dorothy.)

117

A few samples of the trouvailles which came so easily to these painters—Jane, Georgette, Dorothy—and to Solita and Janet who are not painters:

My sleep was made of paper
His glance, blue and brief,
A face unfolds its petals
Like a picture on the air
My life was a buried statue
A nun like moonlight and white stone
The sky is blind with snow
The river is as hard as the road
The swallows fly in circles, with pointed cries
He lay in the position of a child with a sorrow
We weren't treated like people but like migratory thistledown

Georgette said of writing poetry: "A poem, for a poet, is not merely a literary impulse but an urgent and veritable necessity. A poet lives, enclosed, in the silent events which take place between himself and language." And in her prose she wrote like this:

That exquisite hour when night covers twilight, when fragile and poignant relations are established between men and things.

Is the "soul," then, really elsewhere? Since it is my life, how could it have been so outside my human days?

Unless a book is "written," I have little interest in it. And for those plays—like *Waiting for Godot*—which dispense entirely with the act, the art, of literature, I have a zero attention. To me there is nothing in *Godot* to justify the tributes it has received—"Noble and moving," "With phrases that come like a sharp stab or beauty and pain," etc. To me *Godot* doesn't exist.

All born writers, I believe—at least those who are poets —have an aversion for dialectic, which is one of my greatest joys. By instinct they seem to know, as Orage once wrote, that

persuasion by dialectic is not only resistible, but what can be done by its means can be undone by the same means. Instead, born writers tend to overpower, seize, and hold captive . . . Such writing is irresistible, and its effects are permanent; for what is admired is more lasting than what is merely reasonable.

I choose the following excerpts from my writer friends to show how they seize and hold captive:

When JANE created, she wrote like this:

"White"

The hot air of the day stays in the city until night. The long slope of my roof presses the heat down upon me. Soon it will rain. But there is no rest in me: my heart is wandering too far. My friends may still be in the city, but I do not seek them. I will go to the animals in the park. Within their enclosures black shadows of camels lie in the darkness. A great white camel broods in the moonlight, apart from the rest. His lonely eyes are closed and he moves his head slowly from side to side on his long neck, swaying in pain, searching in a dream for his lost world. I have seen a Norwegian ship carrying its carved head through the water of a fjord with such a movement.

Now the high clouds cover the moon. Out on the lake a wind assails the layers of heat. A white peacock sits in a tree, aloof, elegant, incorruptible . . . A light green spirit . . . Across the first thunder he lifts his long white laugh at me like a maniac.

"Void"

I cannot live long in your city: it has no zones of pain for me where I may rest, no places where old joys dwell and I may suffer. It is as empty for me as the honeycomb cliff cities of the Southwest. For I shall not know love again in this or any other place.

And this, for painting. Has any surrealist surpassed it?

> The earth slants up in a plane to the farthest place in the sky. Open mummy-cases in exact rows . . . all the queens of the world, their heads turned to the left, lie listening forever to our words of love, a smile of unbelief upon their painted profiles.
>
> The wind gently lifts them from their caskets, they become tall plume-pens of many colours . . . emerald green, blue, yellow, black, cerise. They write in the sand, something that has been forgotten.
>
> A silent music begins to play . . . the music is under the ground.
>
> A pack of red rabbits comes bounding out of a grove to the right, their ears back, their bodies a straight line of speed. They are stopped in the air. They strain to another leap. They are compelled to remain motionless. A smile of indifference points their faces. They slowly change to glistening fish. They fall into a long line . . . abreast. They close their eyes and swim towards the river, singing softly in the night.

Almost every line contains a trouvaille. I love to imagine a book (on any subject-matter whatever) written entirely in this particular idiom—each sentence a gem of moving, musical, magical imagery; an occasion of rejoicing to me, but perhaps of indifference to today's readers. Solita tells me that she is rereading George Moore's trilogy—"and I feel that I'm the only person still alive who appreciates such studious, dignified, flowing prose from another world, another age."

———

Next, a poem of GEORGETTE's—as simple as air—:

J'ai rêvé que mon âme était source,
fontaine et perpétuel jaillissement.

Je savais les paroles des arbres
et que les feuilles, les fleurs,
se reposent de paraître sans couleurs
la nuit.

Je savais tous les secrets de la terre—
son corps que mon regard ne peut embrasser,
son sang qui anime la sève,
et cette conversation avec le ciel—
échange qui les rend complices.

Mais je me suis éveillé dans les pleures
car je ne savais pas
le premier mot de ton coeur.

(I dreamed that my soul was a welling spring,
a fountain, rising endlessly.

I knew the words of trees
and that flowers and leaves
rest from their colours at night . . .

I knew all the secrets of the earth—
of its body that my eyes cannot contain,
of its blood that quickens the sap,
of its conversation with the sky—
that exchange which renders earth and heaven accomplices.

But I wakened in tears
because I did not know
the first word of your heart.)

(Translated by Solita)

And another by Georgette:*

I had a dream. I walked for years, searching a planet. Across space I arrived. At first I thought that the cities, the people, the things, were like ours. Soon I saw that all was different. People loved one another and they did not speak. The animals spoke.

---

* This dream was not written for a book, but came to me in a letter and I quote it as an example of what the simplest natural writing can be. Of course the influence in the dream was Gurdjieff. We are all only two-centered people. Therefore "empty."

I had a long conversation with a white horse as large as a cathedral. He explained to me his two-dimensional vision and his terrors. He understood that I was burning, and to relieve me he hung his mane like a rain about my body. It was he who explained the celebration of a fête such as does not exist in our world. Three seasons had conquered the fourth. I watched the triumphal return of the troops—regiments of summers of all the countries advanced, flags flying, followed by springtimes and early autumns. They had killed the winters.

They were not accompanied by good and evil. Their songs were like bells, their laughter was like the sunlit sea. To amuse themselves along the way they had disciplined plagues, abolished pain, hunted down calumny. My companion said, "With winter dead, they have killed the inevitable. Now death will be no more than a result—the consequence of not having understood."

Suddenly one of the men fell from high up on to the ground before me. He split in two. He was empty.

(Translated by Solita)

A poem by SOLITA:

"Interval"

The lonely exile on the rock waits:
"Only dust on the hearth now,
Only ash in the heart now—
Remember fires? Remember flames?
Flames from the eyes then
Flames from the fingers then,
And the cunning of the right hand."
(If I forget thee, oh Jerusalem,
May my right hand lose its cunning.)

From the cosmic cloud a crowd and one
Not you; the one who is me.
"Veni, vidi—" But there's an end.
Come! Time to go now

Back to the black cloud now,
All aboard for Nirvana!
All is going, all is gone—Your eyes, your voice, you, me.

From Solita: "I awoke today with a poem in my head—and in Latin." (To the memory of Georgette):

"Quaedam Mortua Loquitor"

Somnium lucis longinquum habui
Somnium vita mea candida erat
Quoque somnia obscura multa habui
Inter somnio meo longissimo
Somnia cincta somnio magno.

Cum somnis meis nunc abdita jaceo
Stellae sunt in nocte sempiterna.

"A Certain One Dead Speaks"

A long dream of light I had
The dream was my white-shining life
And many dark dreams I had
Within my very long dream
Dreams enclosed by the great dream.

Now with my dreams I lie hidden
They are the stars in my eternal night.

DOROTHY—emotions barely suggested behind the light words:

I listened with the tips of my senses to the fair silver-wrapped voices of the women, the low whipped voices of the men; to conversations like flower petals, folding and unfolding to slender foreign compliments, as sudden and graceful as shooting stars . . . It was an evening of three exquisite perfections—politeness, pleasure, and protocol. Yet there was something lacking: there was no emotion. There was no place for it in this rare, high, civilized atmosphere. The design of this kind of life excluded friendship. Its charm was its formality—the delicate excitement of a minuet; a serious subject would destroy the spun-silk quality of our surfaced conversations . . . We reduced climate to clothes. Elegant and swift, we skimmed through polished Paris drawing-rooms.

And this:

> . . . Rows of dipping gondolas; dull gold lantern-light breaking into water; drifting serenades, desperate violins . . . Stone and chains and water, and all the dark music of Venice.

———

A French poem that I love, by Germaine Beaumont. Solita: "Germaine's poem so entranced me that I did this *from* it. I say 'from' because a real translation was impossible in so many ideas and places. She approved it with great cries." (The next to the last verse!)

"Journey's End"

Alone in myself, here I rest
In a strange peace of journey's end.
The silence is deep, the unwrinkled shroud
Holds a vague perfume of past roses.

Of the earth's spaces that once I travelled
Remain only harbors on a map faintly traced.
A flame is now spent, a glow has departed
The universe appears, only to withdraw.

The soul in this closed space is torpid
Renounced, alas, the wish to stretch its wings.
Nothing more will show the peaceful sleeper
Those horizons of the future, pledged to other lives.

Deliverance comes too soon or comes too late.
I wait, composed, in the silence of my haven.

Moreover, by what echo could it be distracted
When already it's been seized in Nothing's vice?

I am in myself, only in myself contained,
Like those treasures buried in dark earth,
Like those noble dead that lie like statues—
Silent markers, pointing out the veiled exit.

But no heraldic crown adorns
A sleeping forehead eternity has glazed.
Now they are unknown who were illustrious
Their hands still clasp the hilts of swords.

Their curving feet in icy metal shod
Chill the greyhound's faithful spines.
Could I have believed that you would arise again
Warriors, the hour of your penitence once ended?

In my turn, see now how I resemble you.
My battle's lost, it's time to sleep.
Let no one sound the trumpet to awake.
Could one better sleep than on a bed of ashes?

Could one sleep better than with eyes a-stare,
In a shade more lovely yet than light?
Eternity already like a river sounds,
The estuary's nets are stretching through the sea.

In an unknown sky turn other stars
As I wait on the bank of the obscure shore.
Leaving the ports that are not of this world,
All sails set, at last the ship departs.

As the clearest example I know of a child's way of seeing,
I quote two paragraphs of Dorothy's remembrances of childhood, in her book, *A Personal History*:

> I waited under the wisteria arbor in Central Park for carriages
> to pass by, and people on horseback and bicycles, and then I

crossed the drive; the policeman who held my hand wore a long blue coat with bright buttons, and a high grey hat, and at last I came to the sheep meadow and my rock.

My rock stood a little back from the path. It wasn't a rock when I climbed it—it was a house and on the top was a little hollow filled with rain where I put my buttercups that I picked in the sheep meadow. There I stood on my rock, looking at the sheep grazing far away. And everything looked big all around me, except the sheep.

It is perfect in every way: the insistent, childlike repetitions of the *Is* and *mys* (instead of *the* buttercups); and only a child who would become a painter would have contrasted the largeness of herself and her rock with the perspective smallness of the sheep.

Sir Herbert Read offers an example of "illiterate" prose of "strong emotional intensity—the rhythm direct, dramatic, expressive":

If it had not been for these things, I might have lived out my life, talking at street corners to scorning men. I might have died, unmarked, unknown, a failure. Now we are not a failure. This is our career and our triumph. Never in our full life can we hope to do such work for tolerance, for justice, for man's understanding of man, as now we do by an accident. Our words—our lives —our pains—nothing! The taking of our lives—lives of a good shoemaker and a poor fishpeddler—all! That last moment belongs to us—that agony is our triumph.

—Vanzetti to Judge Thayer

And Sir Herbert comments:

Though this speech is devoid of all "artistry," of all deliberate structure, it has the elements of great prose. The rhythmical analysis of the passage alone is sufficient to convince one of this. The rhythm mounts in a tempo as triumphant as the mood it expresses; the simplicity and pathos of the words used do the rest.

I have another example of "expression," of an infinite and awful pathos—a letter sent by a mother to her son who, she had just been told, was to be executed the next day:

My beloved son, I have just heard and I can't yet believe it, and I shall pray that something will intervene. I am very strong, my Georges, as I know you are too. I have never been closer to you, and I want you to know that I shall be with you to the very end. I wish I could die with you, but this is not possible. Justice shall be done you, I swear it. Everyone who has known you loves you and admires you, and I, my little one, I am proud of you. Count on me for everything, your head high and your heart pure, my Georges. All honour shall be yours. I place my heart on this paper, which I kiss with my whole soul. Au revoir, my beloved. Think of me at the end, as I shall be thinking of you. Again kisses. Your mama."

I wrote down some night thoughts just as I had recaptured them in the morning, wondering whether they had really "expressed" anything:

I had an experience last night, a mixture of dream, nightmare and illness. I shall remember it as the worst night of my life, worse even than the night of Georgette's death, because then I had moments of relief—she was no longer suffering. Last night, for six hours, I hadn't a single minute of release from visions of horror.

It began at midnight with a crise of seasickness, and with a simultaneous torture that wasn't really dream or nightmare—I was fully awake, sitting in an armchair, bent over with nausea, and finally so weak that I had to slide down to the floor to rest. I heard myself groaning, as the only relief between attacks—six or seven. By this time my mental pain had surpassed physical pain. It went on until nine in the morning.

Visions and images . . . There was a hole dug straight down to the center of the earth. I stood at the bottom of it—the bottom of life—the beginning of the scale of life; I was a statue that had always been standing there, never moving up by an inch. My state was worse than nonentityness—whatever that would be. I was nothing, had no being, no life, no mind, had never had any real emotions, or courage, or unselfishness—just a creature of sloth and greed. You can't imagine the concentrated despair. I began to understand suicide—the need to escape from an incredible hell. I thought, this is worse than being burned alive; yes, worse—there's an end to burning, but there'll be no end to my mental anguish. I'll never be able to forget what I saw myself to be—a person who has no being and who writes glibly about Montaigne's "to know how to enjoy one's own being resembles divinity." I don't see how I lived through all this. A tear began to fall from my eye, as I bent over, and a drop wanted to fall from the tip of my right nostril—I give these details because they seemed so important (if you can believe it)—and I said to myself, "Perhaps I'm not totally dead, these drops show there's at least some organic life in me." Many wild thoughts like this which I can't remember . . . What should I do? I have greatly enjoyed what I thought was my "being," but which was only my capacity of "being happy." Another thought that kept recurring: no one can have anything authentic unless he has experienced what I have tonight. It should be evident from his talk, his judgments, whether he has ever experienced *this*.

I sent these pages to Solita the next day. She answered:

I couldn't speak for an hour after reading your letter, such was its effect. It may be that you, of all of us who went to Gurdjieff, have really had what he meant by the experience of *nonentityness*. Compared with yours, other experiences are academic. Your letter is a marvel of communication and can you not incorporate it somewhere in your ms.? But do not touch it, dress it, cut it. It's perfect, genuine, and would only lose from editing a single word.

After such an experience one has learned something, and what I learned from this one came as a startling revelation, belated and fearful:

I see that all my life I have remained a child.

128

WHAT IS THIS THING CALLED ART?

What is this "strange necessity," this overwhelming love of Art, this dilettante's delight, this raving about beauty? Of what value my obsessions, my manias, my violent appreciations?

A GOOD ANSWER DESERVES A GOOD QUESTION. Therefore:

QUESTION: To what extent is the real meaning of Art accessible to our experience?

Gurdjieff said, "I too was once sick man for Art."

Not as sick as I am, I thought; and hated to think it.

I was sobered by Gurdjieff's statement; for a while I was even aghast, and tried and tried to understand exactly what he meant.

He also said, "Do not love Art with your feelings."

Well, I don't, I reasoned. I love it with my emotions.

"That's an evasion," my opponents argued. "We're tired of your distinctions between feelings and emotions. They're the same thing."

"No they're not. Feelings are of the senses; emotions are —why not say it?—of what is called 'the soul.' "

I began to hold long and tortured discussions with myself. I even imagined that Socrates and I were having a dialogue and he asked, "Shouldn't your 'entirely beautiful' include the true meaning of beauty, i.e., beauty as goodness and truth?"

"Yes, of course. And you once defined beauty as 'the pilot of the soul.' But how dare I suggest that I understand what this means?"

"To suggest is often to persuade."

"I know. But it's hard to talk about what you called 'the upper world.'"

"Yes, but surely it can be attempted?"

"I suppose so, if . . ."

"If you remember that the true order of going is to begin from the beauties of the earth and mount upward for the sake of that other beauty, and to know at last what the essence of beauty is."

In spite of my hallucinatory love of Art, I can at least write of how Gurdjieff's teaching helped me to a different understanding.

First, that Art is not man's highest aspiration, it is merely one of his greatest pleasures. Second, that it is not man's salvation; it does not lead to the evolution of the "soul."

Art as we know it is being-in-love. Consequently not to be taken too seriously.

Being-in-love is a situation of frenzy, trance, or madness. Real love is something else.

Art is also a trance and a frenzy. But, as Gurdjieff said, it began by being something else—a revelation concerning the development of the soul. The Art we know today—have known for how many centuries?—has lost this motivation and message. What should be understood, therefore, is that "art," "beauty," "being-in-love" are subjective states, and that real Art, real love, real beauty are objective states allied to the ancient function—the development of "being."

Today in high circles art is mused about in terms of the "soul." Someone (I forget who, perhaps Paul Klee) said: "Art reveals, by way of the senses, the instinct of the soul; triumphing over intellect, it speaks directly to the heart." Well, it does speak to the heart, as do a thousand other stimuli. It *speaks* to you, it doesn't *teach* you. All that arrives by way of the senses leads to the development of the senses, not the soul.

130

There has been too much vague talk about the "soul." I prefer to remember Gurdjieff's words: "Man has no soul, he has only the potentiality"; and this potentiality is not developed in an obsession, a hypnosis, or a swoon. I must accept this fact—I've lived in a swoon of Chopin since my earliest years, and I know what this state does *not* do for a human being.

To my credit (perhaps) I can say that I've never totally succumbed to my most frenzied "life emotions." If I'm in love—merely in love—and tempted to follow my infatuation to the ends of the earth, I've never done it; I've never even admitted this madness into the *center* of my life (my inner life), knowing in advance the ending of such a story. But when I really love I will go anywhere, even to a country which stifles me, in order "to be where you are." There seems to be a link between Love and the Soul—perhaps that both must be earned. To gain the heart of another you must make yourself acceptable, you must give the beloved first place. To gain a soul you must also become acceptable—give the soul first consideration. In real love, the world-well-lost is easy. But to lose the world to gain a soul . . . this is hard. I know, because I have tried. But I remember Gurdjieff's words, and I keep on trying to make them a reality for me—the reality with a capital R which I spoke of in my fifth Foreword.

"Manifestations." In talking about real love—the "art of love" —Orage often spoke of "the conscious love motive": the lover's wish that the beloved should arrive at her own native perfection regardless of the consequences to him. "It is the fruit of art, of selftraining," and often consists of the lover's ability both to take hold and being able to "let go."

To me, this art of letting-go has always seemed to be within the power of everyone, but the more difficult exercise of "supporting the manifestations of others" seems almost beyond the

131

power of *anyone*. My last conflict over such manifestations began on a Monday morning in 1968.

For a week I had looked forward to a concert on my transistor, at 7:35 on Monday evening. Argerich and Richter were featured together, playing one after the other. Nothing could have made me miss this concert.

But on Monday morning I was still brooding over a criticism made on Sunday of my life, my ideas, my judgments, and my well-known gift for making the right plans. Superficial criticism, lack of awareness and observation, have the power to make me appear unbalanced and push me to self-justification. Yesterday I had concealed my irritation over such interference, but the control had left me fuming and, as usual, "forced" to write a letter of explication. I said to myself, I must write something like this: "If you continue with your plans of trying to influence my life, please discuss them with your friends, if necessary, but conceal such activity from me. As you well know, I have no place in my life for such conflicts. My nervous system can't stand to have things taken out of my hands."

My fuming continued all day, planning just how to formulate a letter. Night came, and I was still "identified" with my exasperation. Exhausted, I looked at my clock: it was 8:15. The concert had been at 7:35.

. . . I had reached across my bed to find the concert program, and when I saw that I had missed the music I became so weak that I fell over on the bed. I was saying (as if screaming), "I've missed it, I've missed it." I tried to get up, finally was strong enough to reach, and drop into, my green armchair. My solar plexus had begun to feel like steel, and someone was hammering on it—"You've missed it." My emotion wasn't in the heart, where the great emotions are supposed to lie; it was an ill-natured emotion—muscular, not heartfelt, but hard and deep, in the solar plexus.

Suddenly a horrifying image took shape. My solar plexus

began to swell. It became so large that it extended from my neck to the seat of my chair—I was sitting on the end of it. And it was no longer steel, it was stronger. As the image continued to swell, this giant plexus became so abnormally strong that I thought, "This is what the Essene monks must have done: developed their emotional centers to such a degree that their other, weaker centers were too dead in comparison to feel torture, which they are supposed to have endured without suffering."

This awful plexus was no longer steel grey, it had become black and was like the crackling shell of a giant beetle—those great June bugs that have always frightened and nauseated me. And as the shell enlarged, the most awful realization came: my arms had been cut off at the shoulders and my legs at the thighs —I was simply this massive black solar-plexus organ that was propped up on a chair and was being hammered by the words, "I've missed it."

(I would have given anything to hear what, and how, these two pianists played, but now I shall never know because I was angry for having been acted-upon, overruled, misrepresented, and unable to support my critic's manifestations.)

When I was strong enough to move (though still drained of real strength) I looked again at my watch. It was ten o'clock. "I can't sleep, I need some kind of pick-up." I made a cocktail, warm—half cognac, half Cointreau. After drinking it I was comfortably burned and felt strong enough to get into bed. Paralyzed, my eyes open, I lay all night looking at the reflected street lights in the garden, and at 6 A.M. I fell asleep. I have no memory of when my arms and legs had become attached again to my body.

. . . All this torment because I have never learned what Gurdjieff taught about "being able to support the manifestations of others . . ." This as the first step of a new state of civilized "being," and the most difficult task of all.

THE ART OF LIFE

To what do you ascribe the happiness of your life?

Well, I've been called "a lovely freak of nature." I don't know of any equipment more suitable, more essential, for a happy and rewarding life than to be a freak of nature.

What exactly has it done for you?

My most galvanic adventures have been so outside of what is known as reality that I myself sometimes can't believe they happened. For instance, the summer we lived in tents on the shore of Lake Michigan, near Highland Park, Chicago. If I hadn't written about it in *My Thirty Years' War*, and if I didn't have snapshots to prove that we did it, I wouldn't be able today to believe that we did. I'm sure it was a unique experience, yet at the time it seemed as natural to me as if people of my conventional bringing-up did such things every day. And the interesting thing is that I've completely forgotten every factual element connected with this marvelous unreality.

Why was it so unreal?

135

Because it was like a child's conception of the possible. It began like this:

I was publishing the *Little Review* in the Fine Arts Building on Michigan Boulevard in Chicago (1915, 1916?). We had no money; we never had any money for the *Little Review* except what trickled in from subscriptions; we were kept alive by the gifts that people so lavishly bestowed. With the latest we had rented a small house in Lake Bluff, a few miles from Chicago on the lake front. "We" comprised Harriet Dean ("Deansie"), who had joined the magazine out of a delirious devotion to its art life, and one of my sisters, who felt that she could provide a common-sense background for my excesses—though I never knew why, since her life seemed to me a confusion: she had married and then divorced, and now she had the responsibility of two babies, no money, and no place to live. Deansie belonged to a rich bourgeois family on Pennsylvania Avenue in Indianapolis (where I too lived before leaving home), in a house next door to Booth Tarkington. (Dean and Tarkington families horrified at her defection to the anarchistic *Little Review*.)

Spring was coming and we couldn't go on paying rent in Lake Bluff. I took a long walk and discovered a lovely stretch of beach between Braeside and Highland Park. "We'll buy some tents and camp here for the summer," I decided quickly. And we did it, after I had spent days convincing the family that we *could* do it.

But how we did it is now a mystery to me. I know we bought five small tents—where did we find the money? We bought long planks to make floors, and each tent was to have an extra length of planks which would make a little porch. How many planks, how many two-by-fours to put the planks on? How many cans (or kegs) of nails? I have no idea. If I could only remember going to a lumber man, or a hardware store, and buying or begging this equipment, I would be more at ease about the condition of my mind. (I suspect, lately, that feeble-mindedness will overcome me at the end.)

Why?

Because I no longer remember facts, only emotions. The camping plan was a great emotion—literally out of this world; and, finally convinced of my sobriety, the family accepted the plan and we began our exodus.

I don't remember how we left Lake Bluff, but I remember the pleasure I took in our possession of five small oriental rugs, one of which would give each tent the necessary beauty. We had bought five soldier's cots, five camp chairs—with what money? As to where we were to keep our clothes, I've not the faintest memory. But I have a clear picture of our moving. We must have hired a horse and wagon (from whom?), because my picture begins with Deansie and me carrying long planks down to the beach. The bluff must have been hundreds of feet high, and the planks were too heavy for us—a fact we ignored. I know it took all day to set the floors (how did we know how?) and to pitch the tents. Then we placed the rugs, the beds and chairs, and then we must have driven back to Lake Bluff to collect clothes, food, sister and babies. One tent was for them, one for Deansie, one for me, one for a kitchen, and one for "Caesar," who called himself the *Little Review* office boy and who would guard the camp on days when Deansie and I stayed overnight in Chicago to bring out the magazine.

Two dates only are engraved on my mind: our move was made in May and we lived on the beach until November 14, because that was the day I took my last swim. Long before this, sister and babies had had enough of nature and had moved—where? And I had long since discarded my plan of asking the Mason & Hamlin people to send a piano to the beach . . . I could have kept it in my tent, but finally I must have had the sense to consider this plan excessive.

You really thought of such a thing?

I really thought of it seriously, and could have arranged it, I'm sure. There seems to have been no limit to what I could think of and what was usually possible. But there are certain questions which I ask myself today and to which I find no answers—questions that never occurred to me at the time:

Why were we allowed to set up housekeeping on a stretch of public lakeshore? Why didn't the authorities demand our withdrawal? Where were the policemen who should have appeared, threatening us with arrest for illegal tenancy? We never expected them. Why didn't the tents blow down in the violent midwestern summer storms? Why didn't thieves appear in the daytime, when we were all in Chicago, and steal the orientals? Why didn't gangsters or sex maniacs come at night, when Deansie and I were often alone, and rape us? We never gave such fantasies a thought. I remember coming out from Chicago at midnight, during a heavy storm, and discovering by lightning flashes that we were walking in the lake rather than on the beach. Why didn't my one suit—a dark blue serge—become sodden in the rain and unfit to appear in next day? I've no idea, though I vaguely remember patting it into shape and hanging it on a cord in my tent; and I remember that my one crêpe blouse could be washed without needing to be ironed, and that people in Chicago said, "How immaculate you always look." *

To return to your illegal tenancy. You literally defied the law . . .

I defied nothing at all. I ignored the law because I didn't know it existed. It didn't occur to me that anyone would want to curb my inspiration.

---

* I've been challenged about this statement, but it is literally true. Some Chicago manufacturer had produced a new material called I never knew what, but it was off-white in colour, rather crêpy in texture, and it didn't even need all night to dry. It was expensive, but we decided that whatever money was in the *Little Review* till should be spent for such an economy in laundry. After washing, it looked as fresh as the day it was bought.

No one ever tried to?

Well, I had forgotten it until Lois (my sister) reminded me the other day. It appears that one intrusive policeman did venture to approach and announce that we must dismantle the camp. But I'm told that I introduced him to the babies and explained that their health depended on the lake breezes. Being Irish, he was moved and left us in peace.

The things I clearly remember are sunrises and sunsets, camp fires, potatoes baked in ashes and corn roasted over embers; dishes cleaned in sand and rinsed in the lake; hours of observing nature as if I had never seen it before; swimming at sunrise and midnight; grandiose plans for the *Little Review's* future; and hours of leisure for reading poetry and listening to music on our handworked victrola. I remember arriving at the beach one evening and finding that Ben Hecht and Maxwell Bodenheim had left poems pinned on my tent. And I remember the day when reporters from the *Chicago Tribune* came to interview me about the camp, the *Little Review*, and my future plans. I enjoyed talking with them and must have given them a great deal of material I didn't intend to, because the next Sunday we were surprised to find our pictures on a full front page of the book section, and a startling article about our "Nietzsche colony" (these were the days when we were running a series of Nietzsche articles in the magazine).

Weren't you ever worried about winter coming on?

I think I never worried about anything in those days; my superstition was that everything would come out right if you believed it would. Of course it's necessary to have common sense.

You claim to have common sense?

Of course. What can be more sensible than to dominate circumstances? So, you see, I didn't worry, and how right I was. My memory is dim about packing up in November and leaving our paradise, but I remember moving into a house in Chicago which some kind man had lent us for the winter. For the rest, all I can swear to is that I regarded our escapade as a matter of course until the other day, recounting it to someone. I had never reflected that it was really quite exceptional. Pure "art of living."

Did you have other adventures as fantastic as this one?

Oh yes, everything that happened had an aspect of unreality.

You talk about it all very lightly. Considering the tragedy of many lives, didn't your life seem to you rather light-minded?

Quite the contrary. You can only work with the nature given you at birth. My life went as it did not because I was light-minded, but very serious indeed. Otherwise such extravaganzas wouldn't have been possible. Intensity was the requisite, and I have always been intense about everything except the acquisition of knowledge. I was sure that I already possessed enough important knowledge for a lifetime, so it wasn't surprising that the next period of my life was spent in moralizing, proselytizing, urging others to follow my ideas. What *was* surprising—ten years later—was the painful and practical period during which I had to learn of a different and higher aim. My chronic intensity propelled me into this struggle with atomic energy, and I found myself in a spiritual environment as strange to me as outer space would have been.

Intensity can't have been enough to account for your experiences. What other natural gifts contributed?

To me the moral of such a story is that anything you very much WISH can be achieved if: 1) you believe that poverty is merely a state of mind; 2) if you never give up getting what you want; and 3) if you realize (with Blake) that the path of excess is the road to wisdom.

I'm interested in hearing about your moralizing years.

Ah, they are what I most like to talk about.

TRANSFORMATION

I never wanted to live an unembellished life, and I have never done it—I've never had to. Some natural gift for transformation—rebellion, arrangement—made the embellishment possible and helped me to create a "happy fate."

Living under such a compulsion has been like painting pictures of life, and I don't take kindly to suggestions that I might have been less egotistically employed had I become a trained nurse. My friends have enjoyed me more as I am, and I have contributed (what a conceited thing I'm about to say) to their moral rather than to their physical euphoria. Odious as I may sound, this is the truth; and why not tell it, since it is a fact that has made me so happy for so many years? My friends have always said, "Thank you for our happiness," "Thank you for *your* happiness," "Thank you for your talk, your plans, your interest, your nature, your letters"; "Thank you for making our lives such happy, fruitful ones"; and (that tribute I treasured above all), "Thank you for your existence."

I have always rebelled against the unadorned, the unbefitting, the unawakened, the unresisting, the undesirable, the unplanned, the unshapely, the uncommitted, the unattempted—all leading to the unintended. I believe in the unsubmissive, the unfaltering, the unassailable, the irresistible, the unbelievable—in other words, in an art of life.

From 1914 on, the memories that have marked my days are not those of having lived through two monstrous, unnecessary world wars. Instead I was waging and winning battles that are fought for ideas.

These struggles and conceptions led me to construct a code of "perfect" human behaviour. And of course such majestic ideas led people to complain that my world had no meaning to them —"It's not real," they said. Well, I lived day after day in this flawless unreal world, and all I can say is that it was real to me and to my friends. It was based on the concept that there exists an imperishable "ideal" to which one's daily life can approximate; and that in the great human conflicts, no matter how difficult, you can always at least try to keep your *actions* perfect. You can even succeed.

Consider how stimulating it was to believe that the emotions of life can be moulded into the impulse and purpose of art! If you experiment with such consciously directed action you can feel at least as proud as if you were a guided missile, which, the scientists say, behaves as if it had purpose.

I was naïve enough to believe that people could be changed by listening to great theories, that they would act upon them at once, and that there was no reason for a separation between theory and practice. Georgette and I had faith in these illusions and, though Jane had not, we all three wrote letters to the young, to the bourgeois, to those we called the "unknowing," to poets in revolt, to anyone who wanted to ask questions. I never doubted that we had the answers.

Such letters, I now see, can still be evaluated as in advance of their time. Although they were written years ago, their ideas are still in advance of what certain natures can accept and assimilate. These natures must *wait*, and learn from life instead of, in advance, from ideas. I wondered what my life would have been if I had waited.

Georgette once wrote a letter to a young student which I considered a great human document:

I should like to make a conte out of what I was talking about the other evening as we left Chartres . . . of how difficult it is not to love *humanly*, but to follow the subtle directions which rare people demand of us—the rare people who, alone, interest us. I followed these directions all my life with Maeterlinck, but on a single theme—an eternal theme, elementary enough: that of liberty or non-liberty; to respect the space of the other, or to restrict it. However cruel the problem, it shouldn't even be posed. It is scarcely subtle, it is a torture pure and simple that we impose upon ourselves the moment we respect our love and wish to preserve it.

Now I understand many other laws. It is certain that every rare person carries within himself his own laws, which he himself can scarcely define because they are a part of his nature. It is for those who love him to decipher, and to follow, these laws. A really special human being eludes us for a long time, perhaps forever. We know him first only in those instants when he gives us his love, his tenderness. These instants of him are like a faint design made with tracing paper.

The rare person is revealed to us only by the quality of the air which is native to him. It is for us to understand the quality· of this air, to create the conditions favourable to this revelation. It is a science—no, an art, the most difficult and disinterested art. We wish always to produce the revelation, but if we wish it in a manner too positive, or too interested, we prevent it.

One must always be prepared, in love, to lose what one is most attached to.

"Vouloir à la limite du renoncement"—and in such a way that even if the "absence" of the other seems flagrant, no deception closes us in or isolates us from him.

143

When our love is purely physical, sex is the magic door through which we are most sure of finding a mutual magic.

When our love has both body and spirit, there is compensation. When the "revelation" is not there, the body is an aid. It is also a cause of anguish; a torture of the entrails as well as of the plexus. But here, at least, is a visible handwriting! How it reassures us, even as it snatches all from us. This handwriting is the signature of all that eludes our analysis. It is the evidence of magnificence in our blood.

When our love is only spirit, vibrations, union of atoms, we live it as if we were balancing, in a dream, on a tightrope that is not there.

And I remember another letter, short and very simple, which she wrote to a young friend who found it hard to understand the complex personality of a man we greatly admired, though we often found him redoubtable:

We all know that B. is monstrous. I believe, even, that I owe one of the material tragedies of my life to his machinations. But I never think of this when I am face to face with him. For me it is really as if he were two persons—an unconscious monster and a conscious brain.

I never forget; but, when I am with him, I never address myself to his human side. I don't even think of doing so. I see, facing me, only an astonishing mind; so astonishing that its superiority can separate it totally from the human being that he is.

I have the impression that this separation is not total for you. You think of the other side—of the person you know—as much as you think of the person you are listening to. It is this that creates a latent disaccord between you.

Great behaviour is a thing to be worked at, as a pianist works to become a virtuoso.

There is nothing in human relationships I so hate as pressure; and next, impatience—the kind imposed by one person upon another by an abrupt, heavy silence calculated to stifle the conversation. This silence leaves you stranded—which is unfair, since your mind had been invited to function. Such silence becomes pressure.

Am I too exerting pressure when I criticize the silence? I don't think so, I think I am applying FORM. One doesn't enter an argument with another mind unless one is willing to follow a certain code of behaviour—a code that can be defined as ORDER.

If the conversation goes on too long, or is without quality, you are bored? Of course; but you must behave responsibly, you must adjust; you can think of something else while your friend runs on; each must have his own way, his own say; you must have patience. Order can't be achieved without patience, and if you don't like order you don't like art.

In a perfect friendship, conversations don't go on too long. Each friend has learned something about quintessence, and this assures quality. It's like the difference between good writing and great literature: an extra element—something rare, unimagined by anyone else—enters the situation: the element of art.

Great friendships don't happen every day. They happened to me five times in fifty years. The first time, the friend I found was in advance of me, and it took me a long time to catch up (if I ever have). (No, I haven't.) The third time we were equal. The fourth time *I* was ahead and she caught up. The other two times we were delicately balanced; sometimes one was ahead, sometimes the other.

Over the years I learned five important lessons about behaviour from these five friends:

From Georgette: Don't allow yourself to make automatic, mechanical, unconscious exclamations of impatience.

From Dorothy: Don't let your silences (of disapproval, irritation) become loud.

From an unnamed friend: Don't fumble physical gestures.

From Solita: Do your "thinking-out-loud" at home.

From Jane: Make a daily habit of self-observation.

COMMUNICATION

Though we spent most of our *Little Review* years writing about art, in a way contemporary critics never wrote—and, may I say, don't write today—it was our psychological ideas that I considered even more in advance of our time. For example, in an analysis of Joyce's "Exiles" in the *Little Review,* Jane said things about human communication not to be found in Freud, Jung, Adler, or any of the others; and it amuses me to think that Joyce himself, though he wrote the play, would probably never have *talked* about it as lucidly as Jane did. I wouldn't know where to turn today for the kind of insight she showed in her article, and I'm willing to wager that Joyce never would have thought of the interpretation Jane put into the last lines of her first paragraph which I also quoted part of in *My Thirty Years' War:*

> There are people, a few, always the artist I should say, who inspire such strong love in all who know them that these in turn become inspired by love for one another. The truth of the matter is that such a person is neither loved nor lover but in some way seems to be an incarnation of love, possessing an eternal element and because of it a brooding, a clairvoyance of life, and a disdain. In other people he breeds a longing akin to the longing for immortality. They do not love him: they *become* him. Richard is one of these.
>
> . . . The conflict of the play is the conflict of quality. This quality . . . can best be compared to fine- and coarse-mesh nets. A person equipped with a fine-mesh net catches impressions, emotions, realizations, whole worlds that easily slip through the mesh of coarser nets. Richard is one of those with the fine-mesh net; his wife and his friend have the coarse nets of the rest of the world.
>
> . . . Where this difference in quality exists, people are literally

"worlds apart," there is no communication possible: exiles. The wife and his friend do not understand Richard's words, his suffering, his motives, his personal aristocracy. Richard understands that they are alike, he does not suffer because they are about to betray him, he suffers because he cannot put upon them his special illumination about life and love; he wants them to act as they could not act, perhaps, in a succession of lives.

Today I have been thinking of Janet Flanner, and of a phrase she wrote to me after Dorothy's death: "You have always been able to create with your friends a special communication —a kind of final language."

This final language is one of the rewards of a life on earth. It produces that special bond of love called friendship.

Of all the categories of love (romantic love, of which I think I know all there is to know; reproduction love, of which I know nothing; and friendship-love, of which I feel I know more than anyone else), it is the latter that most absorbs me now. What are its requisites, what are its rewards, what are its subtleties?

To me, a perfect friendship isn't necessarily founded on a perfect accord with another person. Of my five great friendships —a number that seems to me amazing, considering the requisites of "greatness"—one was composed of those "fine emanations of assent and dissent" that Henry James extols; and it was the dissent that specially delighted me.

In a great friendship both friends must have temperament, or both must lack it. I can't imagine any real friendship founded on the fusion of a temperament and a non-temperament. The two temperaments needn't be alike, but they must be characterized by intensity of feeling (emotion) and passion of mind. In a "perfect" friendship I think the mind always takes precedence over the temperament.

To me great friendship can be defined by paraphrasing Ezra's definition of art: "The whole of great art is a struggle for communication." Substitute "friendship" for "art," and find another noun for "struggle"—because in friendship of this dimension you don't have to struggle for anything; communication is *there*, it has pre-existed as a need and a potentiality in both friends. The definition should read: The whole of great friendship is a need for, and an assurance of, great communication.

What is *great* communication? Something like great art.

If you ask me what I consider the supreme reward in friendship-love, I will answer: its absence of conflict. It may contain challenge, criticism, controversy, the exhilaration of disagreement, but between friends conflict is senseless. It may be all right between the sexes; it is all wrong between friends. Those rages and reconciliations on which lovers seem to thrive are abomination to me.

In romantic love, conflict can be the most exciting of games; in real love or in great friendship, it would be as alien to me as I would feel should I find myself in an asylum. When I examine all the alleged great friendships I know, there isn't one that is free of the strain and boredom of pitched battles, all as unnecessary as war; or free of those silent tensions that are as loud as the roar of war. Perhaps most friends, as well as most lovers, have to accept these conditions. Perhaps they even enjoy them.

Georgette once wrote:

> If I could begin my life over again I should train myself to support certain human vibrations which have the power of silencing me completely. Three classes of people can paralyze me: those who barricade themselves, whose looks, words, gestures, are so many stones fortifying the ramparts; those whose light wit feeds on any material, turning it into firecrackers; and those whose temperaments seek only a jumping-off place and who are at ease only with people who serve as a parapet.

In another book she wrote: "Great ideas are regarded as *objets d'étagères*, they are not *used*. I shall use them." She did, and in the eyes of the world these ideas ruined her life.

To us they made her that human being in whom we could have confidence. She would never betray a great idea; and she would never betray *you* by attributing a wrong motive to your uninformed behaviour; she would always measure how much life you could be expected to understand, how much experience you had yet to live before you could catch up. "Georgette was vast," her nine-year-old great-nephew said, out of a predictive wisdom few adults possess. "Georgette was perfidious," her enemies said, unable to sense her protection of their backwardness, since it was her way never to tell anyone anything his nature didn't demand for itself, or anything he was doomed never to understand. "What ideal human conduct," Solita said, "I would have it written on all the walls."

I know today that even if I live twenty years longer, the chances are that I won't find a new (a great) friend. Why? Because I know too much about the long, long time necessary to build such a relationship—unless it happens that the two natures are of the same emotional age. Otherwise you must have years in front of you to bring about this miracle of communication. But if the miracle happens, it will be all perfection. As Georgette said, "If it were not perfect, it would not *be*."

Perfection—absolute perfection—is what I'm talking about. During the twenty-one years that Georgette and I lived together I never once heard her make a disagreeable remark, exhibit a trace of bad humor, intrude on my privacy or freedom, admonish my way of behaving, show a sign of impatience with me, or speak a word of reproach. If, as Orage said, there are only three ways of influencing people—(1, by magnetization; 2, by competition; 3, by example)—Georgette's way was that of example.

You want me to believe that such extraordinary harmony really existed, and for how many years?

Exactly twenty-one. But no . . . I'm forgetting. She did once reproach me.

149

How? What about?

It was in Le Cannet, the year before she died. Reynaldo Hahn was conducting a concert in Cannes and had asked her to be his guest. Ill as she was, she was determined to accept, and knew that with patience she could produce her usual psychic and physical radiance. Her left arm was paralyzed and her right hand was unequal to doing what she wanted it to do, but she refused all help from Monique and me. After two hours of watching her super efforts I became so worried that I said, "Georgette, you mustn't go on, you'll make yourself ill."

She looked at me carefully, spoke in her usual voice but with a slightly different inflection, and said "Chérie!"

Well, go on . . . What happened?"

I've just told you.

No, you only quoted one word.

Yes, that's it.

But what else did she say?

Nothing.

I don't understand. What did she reproach you about?

Well, think it over. Perhaps you can figure it out.

She went to the concert with our neighbors, since I was too exhausted to go. Reynaldo welcomed her with red roses, calling out to the crowd in his dressing-room, "Make way for Monna Vanna!"

But I spent those gala hours reproaching myself for having reproached her . . . in other words, for attempting to undermine the rock-strength of a temperament bent on accomplishing its aim. Blind, inappropriate, fatuous behaviour—the conflict of conflicts (which I so abhor in my saner moments), and the most harrowing that strong temperaments have to endure.

This was the last time that she and Reynaldo were to see each other, and she had conducted the event as well as he had conducted the orchestra.

LES BÊTISES HUMAINES

This morning I had my coffee at two o'clock—I couldn't sleep because I kept thinking of the impediments to great friendship. Through the long hours of the night I began making a list of those characteristics which, to me, automatically prevent communication.

What I said about agreement between friends being unnecessary isn't quite true, I think. You can dispense with intellectual agreement, but emotional disagreement is likely to be fatal. Though you needn't be alike in nature, or temperament, you must agree on *standards* of emotion. One of the deepest gulfs between people is disagreement on what is POIGNANT. Fictitious tears can be a real barrier—a conclusive embarrassment.

There is also that distinction between what is INTERESTING and what isn't. You must agree on what general ideas are worth the attention of a developed mind.

But perhaps I should begin my list of impediments with COARSENESS. I read reviews of books called "delicate" (like some of those Japanese stories). I buy the book and then: "No, it's brutish and repulsive." The truth is that I feel so "pure" . . . and I'm not ashamed of it, and I don't care who knows it.

But of all the impediments, perhaps I should name first the distinction between conscious and unconscious VANITY. Georgette defined it in writing of Duse: "Vanité—pire espèce, celle qui affiche son humilité." It can throw life so out of gear that there is nothing to do but to stop driving.

Speaking of Duse, I was so exhilarated years ago by Mabel Dodge's encounter with that humility-vanity that I copied a page out of the Dodge autobiography:

151

. . . As we passed the tall carved wooden Buddha standing on the long table against the tapestry, Duse stopped before him and raised her arm, and, emulating his gesture, moaned, "I hear what he is saying—'Il faut se soumettre!' Shall we ever accept it?" . . . She walked on, in her doomed fashion.

(They got on well for a few days, then came a misunderstanding).

All the warm tragedy was gone from her and she was the personification of rebuke. She managed to convey reproach to me with such conviction that I almost felt guilty; but I knew how she misjudged me. Then I realized in a flash how she probably misjudged everything in life.

She thanked me—in a few words spoken with grace and loveliness—but below the surface she poured out her opprobrium and her frustration. Her eyes unloaded a volume of forceful hatred upon me . . . I began to feel anger mounting in me, and indifference. The spell was breaking . . . The next night at dinner she was full of noble beauty with something sacrificial about it. I suppose I looked coldly at her, I don't know. Catching my eyes, she bent a little look upon me to try to draw the light up into my face again, as one does to a sulking child. She had a forgiving smile upon her face and was as though saying, "Now, dear, let's forget it." This made me still more annoyed, for I didn't need her forgiveness. It was too dull, really . . . I must have scowled for she exclaimed, "Non, non, regards-moi avec tes bons yeux." I looked up and smiled to please her, feeling quite the opposite from what she wanted, but she was easily deceived, for her inner workings were not true.

Ah yes, my list should start with UNTRUE INNER WORKINGS, since they are insuperable. If, for instance, you're talking with a rigid, condescending intellectual, never try to influence him in the proper way—that is, by innocence of heart or intensity of feeling. Instead, interrupt whatever he is saying by announcing that you've been reading "A Mithraic Ritual," or some other esoteric work you're sure he doesn't know. He will stop short in admiration and regard you ever after as a personage. He is easily deceived, because his inner workings are false.

Other barriers:

People who don't distinguish between the PERSONAL and the IMPERSONAL. That is, people who think that the use of "I" in any discussion makes it personal, instead of knowing that "personal" means deformation of the argument by side-tracking, change of subject, self-dramatization, hitting below the belt, conversational doorslamming, and so on.

People who don't distinguish between rich PERSONAL INFORMATION and poor personal material; who consider any personal outpouring as authentic as any other.

People who don't know the difference between TALK and CONVERSATION. This category includes all non-listeners, monologists, unsuccessful exhibitionists; those who have no sense of the value of pause, or who listen only to themselves as they wait to leap into brilliance. Benjamin Constant described them—in 1805—for all time:

> Cette femme ne disait pas souvent des mots isolés qu'on pût retenir et citer, et c'était là, selon moi, l'un de ses charmes. Les mots de ce genre, frappants en eux-mêmes, ont l'inconvénient de tuer la conversation; ce sont, pour ainsi dire, des coups de fusil qu'on tire sur les idées des autres, et qui les abattent. Ceux qui parlent par traits ont l'air de se tenir à l'afflût, et leur esprit n'est employé qu'à préparer une réponse imprevue, qui, tout en faisant rire, dérange la suite des pensées et produit toujours un moment de silence.

> This woman did not often come out with a bon mot that could be remembered and quoted, and this for me was one of her charms, since remarks of this kind, however clever in themselves, have the disadvantage of killing the conversation; they are, so to say, shots that are fired at other peoples' ideas and which slay them. People who throw such shafts into a conversation seem to be lying in wait for a chance to employ wit in some unexpected sally, which, while causing laughter, disturbs the general train of thought and always produces a moment of silence.

. . . Next, people who have become LITTLE CRITICS, whose loud intellectual silence and heavy negative emanations can intimidate and subdue a roomful of their betters.

People who TALK DOWN to you. This is a special category, indicating a blind spot that you can never make anyone aware of. If you've tried once, you'll probably not try a second time.

People who CONDESCEND to you. This outrage is based on an unawareness so total that you are sometimes forced to accept a compliment on your good taste as if it had caused surprise.

People who are separated from you by CLASS CODES. This gulf must be ignored because it is a challenge to their self-esteem. You are left defenseless, not willing to face the disaster your comments will cause.

People who don't know what it is to be NATURAL.

People who live on NEWSPAPER AUTHORITY.

People who have no COMMON SENSE.

    "   " have BAD NATURES—lack of simple good faith.

    "   " aren't capable of saying "I WAS WRONG."

    "   " aren't HOUSE-TRAINED.

    "   " who have never learned the meaning of PRIVACY.

    "   " have no JOIE DE VIVRE.

    "   " have no INNER LIFE at all.

And last—but of extreme importance—those people you never want to see, those you never *should* see. They are those who have always been a thorn to anyone who lives for a purpose, and they are prevalent. You describe them simply as "empty" —as if this adjective were sufficient. They are lively and bemused, and usually they consider themselves to be your best friends. They are therefore touching. Not one of them would suspect that I am writing of him (or her) here, and you do your best to keep them from suspecting it. When you are most oppressed by their presence, they feel you are most impressed; when you are most dejected, they feel they have most pleased and entertained you. They are so pleased with the pleasure they think they have given that they can't stop supplying you with it. Nothing you can do or say will arouse them to your nervousness —unless you are willing to say (as you are not), "Please examine your offering and realize what it does to me; and please go away from me before my nervous system betrays me into a convulsion." They continue to regale you while you hold yourself in control, silently searching for a formula that could alert them to your state. What you want to say is: "You are offering me a look into a void, and I have no way of making you understand the difference between this death and the life lived by people who are SOURCES OF LIFE."

My great friends have always been sources of life.

Certain human bêtises belong to a category outside the universal shortcomings listed above. They are the qualities that characterize "bad natures."

Everyone is stupid in some ways, vain in some ways; everyone is selfish, self-centered, self-enamoured, unaware to some degree; and everyone tells lies. But everyone is *not* bad-natured, everyone is not petty, spiteful, bitter, resentful, rancorous, disagreeable, bad-humoured, suspicious, revengeful, tyrannical, vindictive, or treacherous. These are the bêtises that are abominable, unnecessary, and insupportable, and as incurable as a tendency to write bad poetry.

The interesting thing is that you can flairer these bêtises in people you know only by sight. In my daily promenades on the Avenue Victoria I pass a man and his wife of whom I know nothing except what can be sensed by a quick glance as they pass by. I'm sure that the woman is "good," and just as sure that the man has a bad nature. You know it by the studied self-consciousness of his walk, by the strutting vanity visible in the way he swings his arms, by a sort of chip-on-the-shoulder alertness. You know that, day and night, his thoughts are uninterruptedly upon himself, and you don't have to know him to dislike him.

I am always troubled about General De Gaulle. I've been willing to think of him as a "great man," but I like great men who are likeable. That quirk in his nature, those unnecessary complications which he introduces into all situations and which illustrate his disagreeable *way* of doing things, his egoism, his tyrannies, his pettiness and unkindness, his lack of good faith, his vindictiveness, his moments of cruelty would make me flee his personal environment as if the operations of his bad nature could poison my life.

Granting his qualities, I wish I could admire him more than I do. But even if I could, I could never like him.

I like the King of Denmark.

I've had a great deal of "fun" by writing a little comment in the *New York Herald Tribune* in Paris, which they printed under the title "Who Likes De Gaulle?" I had said, "How pleasant and profitable it would be for mankind if De Gaulle had a good nature! Being extremely bad-natured, he lacks the qualities of les hommes de bonne volonté, and even if people admire him I can't understand how they can like him."

This comment was answered by a man close to De Gaulle, and appeared on TV as a short debate: "Who likes De Gaulle? I do, for one; but then, of course, I know him."—Harold King, Chief Correspondent, *Toronto Telegram*, Paris.

So I wrote again:

Mr. King's response to my letter—that he likes him because he knows him—is the kind of riposte I most enjoy, because it can so easily be deflated. In other words he is saying that love is blind. Knowing De Gaulle or not isn't the argument. *Has he or has he not got a bad nature?* He has given a hundred public proofs that he has; therefore privately his friends will be subjected to it sooner or later. I hope Mr. King has no illusions about being spared. It's better to be prepared in advance for the exhibition.

I've been rereading this manuscript and I'm not impressed. It's easy to imagine the public's reaction to these discriminations I've been defining: "So you associate only with extraordinary people, do you? In our opinion ordinary people are more interesting than you are. How can you imagine that what you've written will move or excite us? There's nothing profound, heroic, inspiring, unselfish, or noble in it; there's no wit, no humour, no charm; there's no struggle or hardship, no common human denominator; there's no adventure, no sex, no violence; there's no participation in world problems. You're a preacher, and a boring one. You're a monomaniac, interested only in your own thoughts and feelings, and as far as we're concerned it's just too bad about you."

Well, I'm willing (almost) to agree with them. It was Ezra, I think, who said that any book written with pleasure would be a live book. Of course this isn't true. I've been writing with great pleasure, I can't wait to get up at daybreak and rush to my typewriter; but this doesn't guarantee that my book is alive.

Still, I believe that it has *something*. It's not like those "non-books by non-writers for non-readers about nothing." It has at least a *concern*?

As I reread, my reactions have a pendulum movement. At times I say, "Probably the dullest book ever written." At other times I say, "Entrancing; the kind of book I shall want to read more than once." Later I say, "I don't know a single human being who will want to read this simple, unentertaining book; or who, having read it, will have enjoyed it."

Later still I wonder if I (who feel so unpompous) am perhaps as pompous as those people from whose pomposity I flee. One thing only am I sure of: I *know* I haven't got a bad nature . . . unless we know nothing at all about ourselves—which is probably true.

Confirming my doubts about my writing talent, I had an experience with the *New Yorker*. I had sent them a short sketch about an evening's disastrous drive with some American tourists, and everyone here called it hilarious; so I sent it to the *New Yorker*, convinced that they would agree. They quickly rejected it—"Very sorry this didn't work out here." This tempted me to argue with them. "But didn't you think it was funny," I asked, "didn't you laugh at all?" "No," they answered. "Terribly sorry; it may be something is wrong with our sense of humour, after all." "Must be," I answered, and that ended our repartee. But I still think it's a funny story:

Drove to Mougins with three nice American tourists. Huge American car, I in front with the driver.

Never again will I drive with Americans. If I had dared to speak, these are the words they would have heard:

Stop screaming, stop speaking, CONTAIN yourselves. Put your attention on the car, stop making faces, stop gesturing, stop *moving*; it's as if you were doing an Indian war dance before my worn-out eyes. Stop jerking, have you never heard of "pulling yourselves together," can't you feel that my organism is writhing, have you never learned anything about silent, private functioning? What would you do if I should scream and begin to jump up and down in the front seat so that you couldn't drive? Stop the car, let me out or I'll be sick and then you'll realize what you're doing to me. Don't talk of any and all things while you're driving, close your mouths, keep your eyes still, hold your hands still, don't ask me questions about where we are and what I like to eat, don't tell me disjointed stories about your family life at eighty miles an hour, don't ask me if we can have vol-au-vent for dinner, don't mention what you ate last night and what it cost, don't say "Excuse me" when it's not necessary, don't chuckle, don't guffaw, don't yell, don't tell me another newspaper headline, don't keep turning your eyes in all directions, look at the road, don't comment about anything, especially literature—you're supposed to be driving a car, a car is a machine to be handled by experts, it's not a social situation, we're not at a party, don't ask me if I've read Cummings or you'll hit that car ahead, don't entertain me with another comparison between French and Americans, don't utter another truism about anything, tone down your voices, at whom are you shrieking, why these piercing cries? Look at my face (without turning your head), can't you see I may faint, can't you feel the wrath rising in me?—the force of it should appall you! How much longer must I stand this, have you never suspected anyone's inner devastation caused by your unawareness of all that is driving me mad? If you continue I shall have to hit you. Keep still, stop the car, let me out, don't look puzzled or incredulous, surely no action of mine can shock organisms like yours, I just want to get out and away from you . . .

After dinner—(all this went on from seven to eleven P.M.)—they drove me back to my peaceful house. I fell on the bed, my neck began to throb with agonizing pain, my head filled with terrifying electric wires, all buzzing and crackling. I got up, went downstairs, almost fell, made coffee, couldn't control leg muscles which became too rigid to get up the stairs. Never, never again will I allow nice, kind, generous Americans to enter into my contained life.

And to think that I sat through these four hours looking happy, putting them at their ease, stimulating them through dinner to the point that they couldn't bear to say goodbye. How long will it take me to re-enter my own world and take up my lovely, lonely life again? (Writing all this to you has made me feel sane, and the electric current in my head has been turned off.)

Last comment: they were observant in one way: one of the men never handed me back my pen-pencil without carefully pushing the point back in.

FREEDOM

To continue with unenlightened behaviour.

I once kept a sort of diary-journal. Its subject? That most rare of all felicities—FREEDOM.

Once upon a time, long ago, I lived for a few years without freedom. I made efforts during those years to adjust to a way of life that wasn't my own. You do this because you love someone, because you want your friend to be happy. You are willing to do it for months, not for years. And you always hope that sooner or later you can make the person you love understand your need of freedom—and, you hope, hers.

Don't hope. If freedom isn't there in the beginning it will never be there. No one ever understands the idea, the need, or the feel, of freedom who doesn't start with the need as ultimate.

I like to reread the desperate pages of that diary written during my struggle to recapture the freedom I had lost.

I could never understand why two individuals living under one roof couldn't live like two individuals under two roofs. But I never saw it happening, and I never see it happening today. I had come to believe that it never *did* happen, and then I met Georgette and found that it did. I discovered that freedom is the simplest of mysteries if you are simple enough to understand it, to crave it, to deserve it, and to offer it; and of course intelligent enough to recognize that certain lacks of freedom are inevitable, but acceptable as long as you have the one freedom that is important. Which is simply the freedom to *feel free.*

I never talk of freedom as a demand to have one's own way. No one can have his own way. No one can escape adjustments, concessions, the welcomed responsibilities of love. But if you can *feel* free, even while you adjust and concede, you are saved.

The only hope of such freedom (which I call "perfect" freedom) lies in the super-awareness possessed by a rare person who knows how to make others feel free. It is a gift of purity; purity of nature, like pure intelligence or pure goodwill. It saves you from embroilment in the human bêtises.

I have never heard anyone say that his personal life, in relation to another's, was free. Let anyone who disagrees examine his own life and then say whether, in all situations, he feels free. The answer will always be NO. But Georgette and I *did* feel free, and we felt it in spite of differing temperaments and idiosyncrasies. And neither of us ever found it in relation to anyone else.

During my unfree years I often sat up all night writing out my rebellion. And for these night thoughts I borrowed a phrase of Heathcliff's—applying it to life, not to love: "I cannot live without my life."

I wrote a letter about my distress:

I am living as you want to live. It has become the opposite of the way I want to live. If I go on I am under sentence of death.

I'm *down* in my inner strength, and I can't build it up again unless I can live alone for a while. For three years I've been available at all times. I'm not really an available person. I'm willing to be available at intervals; then I must be unavailable at intervals.

After a few days of communal living, I must have a rest from it. I can no longer be a unit with anyone; I am myself, separate; I must again become the master of my own impulses. If not, I begin to disintegrate.

I have never known, or heard of, a family that had freedom. I have never known a mother, a father, a child, grandchild, grandparent, aunt, uncle, sister, brother, friend, husband, wife, lover, who was, or who felt, free. And their fenced-in suffering is always non-existent to their tormentors. I know people so sensitized to physical suffering, or to many kinds of psychic suffering, that the slightest flicker across a loved face calls out their total protection. But the special psychic suffering of the unfree, as visible as violent light, is always invisible to those who fear the idea of freedom, who fear that if others are given freedom they will be uncapturable.

Freedom is the only bond that could ever utterly bind me to another human being.

Something is gnawing at my life—my wonderful life which I have steered so competently away from the life-sentence of communal living.

You deny that there is any pressure on me. Why should I feel it if it isn't there? You say, "Why don't you do as you like? I don't interfere with you, I allow you every freedom."

Is *that* what you understand by freedom? One doesn't *allow* freedom; it would be like allowing *life*. Freedom must be like Everest . . . simply be there.

The pressure of an unconscious demand upon me—unspoken but felt through walls—depletes me, consumes me. There's a basis of vampirism in such a situation. Why do I suffer so under it? Why can't you understand that I do—why *can't* you, when you've heard me express my anguish so clearly? I don't vampirize you, I do the opposite. But this opposite doesn't make you happy, it is just what you don't want. You want life always to be personal. Can I make you understand that I don't? No. Because everyone understands only those experiences he has already experienced. You have never wanted to be alone, and free.

You attach no strings, you say. Well, if no strings are attached, no strings are felt.

And then there's that other insidious factor in the life-sentence of domestic living—the fact that the movement of daily living takes precedence over the movement of thought. Will I ever recover from the mental sluggishness into which I fall when, to avoid tensions, I must eliminate all conversation which might develop into that "scornful vigour which incites the heart" and revivifies the mind? You offer, instead, monologues on subject-matter which has already been thoroughly masticated. When I try to escape into discriminations, observations, fantasies, eccentricities, impersonalities, a feather-bed is thrown over my head. Why? Because such escapes would free me from personal living, would even allow me time to write a book. But you say, "That would take all your time, what would *I* be doing?"

I say, "Why can't we at least live a half-domestic, half-professional schedule—give the mornings to uninterrupted concentration, the afternoons to errands and all the other boredoms?"

"But I write from nine to twelve. I concentrate, nothing interrupts me. Why can't you?"

Because we measure time differently. You measure it in physical units; you have three physical hours in which your mind functions. I haven't. I have the same three hours, but they are measured in psychic units. The first hour I spend in recovering from yesterday's pressures—an hour during which time whirls around me in a madness of speed, and I can't stop the vibrations in my solar plexus. It's like being an ocean liner whose engines have been stopped a long time before landing, but the ship still moves forward on its acquired momentum. By the second hour I have become still and can begin to think. By the third hour I've come upon my conception, and then—just as I begin to write—it's lunch time, and that is sacrosanct. You have had three hours of work. I haven't had one.

I feel that I'm encased in glue, and I can't make the movements of getting out.

If I speak of my dilemma you call it an argument and say, "Let's not belabour the point." I don't need to belabour it; one statement should be enough. What should I do when a visible desperation isn't enough? When a steamroller crushes me and my flattened state isn't even noticed? When I look and feel ill because of my astonished suffering?

My private existence has been drained away drop by drop. My nature no longer has any place in the life we're living—it is not welcome. As a result my nervous system lives on in a helpless, hopeless brooding, from which I can emerge only by recording these rebellions in the night.

It has become too much for me—this being forced to resort to, and deal with, the behaviour of childhood.

But at the other end of this tunnel came the years when I was free again to impose my own ideas. And it was this turning point that gave my life an aura of the unearthly.

163

I read an astonishing statement the other day: "We now have a paralyzing knowledge of the degree to which our subterranean selves govern our motives and conduct."

I would say that we have no knowledge about ourselves, especially subterranean, and that anyone who has watched Gurdjieff at work on our brilliant psychiatrists would learn that there exists a kind of knowledge about which such analysts know nothing. "Conscious" knowledge.

After you have studied a few years with Gurdjieff you will have learned a great deal about the "position" of people; a hundred revealing signs indicate what rung of the ladder (in respect of conscious knowledge) they stand on. You begin to feel that you can understand their essential natures. You say: this person is at the stage where he suspects that he isn't what he thought he was; this one is at the stage of fixed vanity and illusion that nothing can influence; this one may be aware that such hierarchies exist, but scorns such knowledge; this one believes in such knowledge and hopes to learn about it; this one is a "simple man" who can be helped by revelations.

This immediate evaluation must be rather like the "colour of one's aura" of which initiates speak. I'm not at home in such terminology. I have merely observed Gurdjieff's application of his science of types, his exact knowledge of the human psyche.

Someone will say, "I understand what you mean. You're talking about what any competent businessman knows; he must be a judge of character." I am not, I say. I'm talking about *conscious* knowledge. There are no "conscious" businessmen.

Conscious knowledge is always surprising, even astounding.

You may think you have judged someone's character precisely, you're sure he's an upright, modest, generous, trustworthy person. Then you watch Gurdjieff "step on his corns"—which was his expression for an attack on the Achilles heel. You see a different person emerge. You are shocked; you begin to realize how distant this type of knowledge is from all the psychology we know.

As you grow more conscious you wonder how Gurdjieff, knowing our poor characters so completely, could put up with us at all. One pupil said, "You have much patience, Mr. Gurdjieff." "No," Gurdjieff answered, "much practice."

Conscious knowledge saves time and energy otherwise expended on false hopes, illusory expectations. And it makes for loneliness. One of the first things Gurdjieff told us was this: "You will sometimes feel as lonely as a louse in the middle of the ocean."

I have not yet felt so lonely as that, I suppose I haven't yet felt deeply enough for that. In any case, I would rather be lonely alone than lonely with others, or with one other. This is why I no longer offer my inner life to the world at large, as I always did when I was young. Today I show people only my outer fringes; then, if they look interested, I show at least some aspect of my inner self. Those who seem to like it, or want it, at once ask for more. Others show quickly that they don't like it, don't understand it, and find it de trop; therefore with them I don't try again. I know that between them and me nothing will ever transpire. I simply say to myself, "There is no use in my 'being' being here."

And then what? I practice the most boring of all human exercises: I say "Yes?" and "Really?" I let them talk without interruption. I say "How interesting!" or "I don't quite understand what you mean." They explain, usually at length, and I smile, and they smile, and we get on well together. We quote to each

165

other the latest headlines we have both read in the morning papers. I can do this now as well as the next person, but I would die of inanity if I had to keep it up.

The interesting thing is that, since I've become uninteresting, people like me better this way than the way I used to be.

I'm being insufferable again, I suppose. But, as Frank Lloyd Wright once said, "Why not a little honest arrogance from time to time?"

Solita says that she now never shows her inner life to anyone. It is difficult for me to take this statement literally. I think she means that she's still sometimes willing to show it, but rarely, and usually on paper.

I haven't yet come to this silence. There are still three people to whom I never show anything but my inner life, valueless as it may be . . . Stop, stop! How easy it is to lie! I think it is valuable and interesting. All right. Then I should say that with at least three people I still proceed on the premise that I would rather never see them than deliberately subdue my exaltations.

Living alone, today, my inner life has spaciousness, as it had when my two lovely companions were alive. I have never since then found real spaciousness anywhere else, except here alone with Monique. Even with my two closest and dearest friends today I sometimes have to subdue myself, hold back, walk on eggshells. It's as if there were something too strong in me which I don't want to thrust upon anyone. Besides, I don't particularly enjoy this feeling of too much strength, I don't need it. Unless I keep something of myself to myself I hear Solita say, "Why don't you give up your verbal explosions? They may not deplete *you* (you think) but they may (do) deplete others."

They have not depleted all others. But of course I could give them up; only my spaciousness would go with them, and I love the only voyages into space I shall ever make: my own.

It was from Gurdjieff that we learned a great deal about what he called "objective" behaviour, and this gave me new opportunities for moralizing—usually in a pompous way:

Dialogue—with an unhappy young wife:

> *She* : My husband doesn't love me, he no longer loves me.
>
> *I* : Why keep on saying that? Why not say, "He isn't happy"?
>
> *She* : If he doesn't love me I can't make him happy. That's what I'm concerned about—his happiness.
>
> *I* : No, you're not. You're concerned about your own.
>
> *She* : ! ! !
>
> *I* : When you're identified with someone you always say HIM when you mean ME. Identification is a deadly business. Can't you imagine that your husband's happiness doesn't depend on you alone?
>
> *She* : No.
>
> *I* : Look out the window at that man passing in the street. You don't know him, therefore his happiness doesn't depend on you; but he may be a happy man. In a way, your husband is like that stranger—his happiness doesn't exist only in relation to you. But you won't detach yourself from him, you refuse to look at him as a human being with a life apart from your own. Why do people behave better toward someone they don't love than toward the person they "love"? Because they aren't identified with the one they don't love. Identification is evil, it prevents you from understanding the other person. A great man is one who understands others, and this is the "impartial love" that Gurdjieff talked about—"love as a key to being," "objective love." *This* is higher morality. But you're not interested in it; you're interested only in keeping your husband. You will lose him . . . unless you can

learn to understand that aspect of his entity which is entirely independent of you.

Today I wouldn't preach at such length.

I've just heard of two friends who are fighting the same old battle of "You have no right," etc. What amazes me most in the human comedy is that people never seem to know that they're in it, and never get tired of living it at its most intensive heat, as if their involvement in it were something new and strange. So today I wouldn't say more than this: "I should like to shock you both—one for being jealous and DARING to show it; the other for not insisting on freedom and privacy, and OBTAINING it."

Orage: Great love can both take hold and "let go." In conscious love each lover delightfully works perfection in the other. But this state is not ordinarily attained in nature; it is the fruit of art, of self-training.

Love without knowledge and power is demoniac. Without knowledge it may destroy the beloved . . . "I love you," says the man. "Strange that I feel none the better for it," says the woman.

Conscious efforts to anticipate the nascent wishes of the beloved while they are still unconscious are the means to conscious love. The conscious love motive . . . is the wish that the object should arrive at its own native perfection regardless of the consequences to the lover.

Such love always begets a similar love in the object. Conscious love begets conscious love.

THE ART OF LOVE

THE LIFE OF A GRAVE

Nineteen forty-one . . . On a quiet evening in October, Georgette's life came to its end. Her tawny eyes opened and looked up at us for the last time. Then she sighed gently, and died.

She lay in the room where I am now writing, and I sat beside her in the night and held her hand. As the hours passed I imagined I was hearing Chopin's Twentieth Prelude played as I suddenly knew it should be played.* The twelve great measures, taken at a new tempo, in a different rhythm, filled the room and the night—played more slowly, very slowly, as if with each measure the hands that touched the piano were enfolding the departing presence. Each chord was taken on a count of three, as if this were the only rhythm in which a farewell could be conceived. Ever since that night I have waited in vain to hear someone play it like this.

---

* See page 70.

. . . We walked down the hill behind the white hearse covered with white flowers. In the church the organist was playing Bach's "Viens, douce mort"; then the Bach Chorale, "I Call upon Thee, Jesus"; and Chopin's saddest Etude.

In the little Cannet cemetery we filled the waiting grave with tuberoses. Around it were nine small graves, each with a tombstone marked "Notre cher petit ange." Monique, with her poor bent back and desperate face, stood rigid and immovable, throwing her tuberoses long after it was time to move away. Someone touched her arm, but she pushed his hand away as if defying the whole world to stop her, and went on throwing, throwing. Then we left Georgette there, under the sky, beneath a mound of white flowers, for all the nights to come.

Perhaps one shouldn't try to write about death. The silence of those who hold this theory has often impressed or moved me, but it has never satisfied me. Alice Toklas quoted Gertrude Stein's last words and then wrote just one sentence: "They took her to the operating room, and I never saw her again."

I prefer Isak Dinesen's idea: "All sorrows can be borne if you can put them into a story, or tell a story about them."

. . . In the Chalet Rose, the days that followed Georgette's death were—to my surprise—days of thought. I was conscious of being preoccupied with something beyond deprivation, and I soon realized what it was. I needed to make an impersonal survey of the fact that for years I had known a unique human being; that I had been aware of this fact daily; that I had watched this human being live and die, as if I knew in advance that such observation would one day serve me; and that it was serving me now, with this strange necessity to clarify what I had found unique in her. To do so, and to do it clearly, became an obsession that filled my days and my nights.

First I had to ask myself whether I was simply doing what everyone does after a great loss—exaggerating virtues, even imagining qualities that hadn't existed. I knew I wasn't, but how prove it? Such an effort would be difficult and it would be unimportant; but it would be comforting. Therefore why couldn't I write down my thoughts as one writes music—not to prove anything but simply to say something?

What appeared "unique" to me was the twofold aspect of Georgette's endowment—that of exceptional human being and exceptional artist. But can this combination be called unique? I could, for instance, imagine that Marc Chagall is such a human being: a type that is serious, but always with lightness; never solemn or heavy; incapable of unkind thoughts or bad faith or pettiness of any kind; the artist engagé in the sense of being both optimistic and pessimistic—optimistic about human progress and pessimistic about his optimism; involved in "helping people," but never undertaking a "great work"—like aiding the natives of Africa or urging nations to stop their wars (knowing that they won't); tempted to propaganda but knowing its uselessness, and always believing that Art is the real, the great, persuader. Of course I didn't know anything about Chagall's daily life and behaviour, but after meeting him, watching his face and sensing that he was "un être tout en vibration" (as Georgette said of Joyce), I imagined that I knew his category and that it might resemble Georgette's. If it did—and there must be others—I would have to relinquish my argument for "unique."

And in fact I soon gave up the effort to prove any such thing. It was a silly ambition, of interest to no one. Who wants proof of anything so outside the great practical issues of life? Very few—except people like me.

Writing today, I am remembering my thoughts as if I had been thinking them continuously during all these years—as I have. However, I realized that if I wanted to write about them now, vitally, the form most assured of vitality would be a journal. But since I've never kept a journal intime, any attempt to use that form now would lead to falseness.

A more natural form for me would be that of a letter—the kind of letter you write unselfconsciously but which, because it is true, holds a reader's attention; the kind you can read aloud afterward without embarrassment, because it won't have the tricky atmosphere of having been written to impress.

Once I've made my decision about form, I thought, my real difficulties will begin. I must write no single sentence that doesn't present an experienced fact—real or that *really* took place in my imagination; I must resist all insertions of hindsight; I must omit much of what I most long to say, pare it down to what I actually did say. In this way, though my recital may not move me, it is almost certain to move my reader. But what is the criterion of "moving"? I think it is this: if my letter keeps to the truth and nothing but the truth, I may or may not succeed in writing well, but I will have written in a way to capture attention. If I read the letter aloud to someone I won't have to watch his eyes wander away from me. This in itself is proof of a good style. It won't be "fine writing" (to be avoided in any case); it won't perhaps be eloquent, and it won't be comparable to what a real writer could do with my material. But it will be clean writing, it will be my truth, and there's a chance that it will be moving.

After I've got this far, I must pass three other tests. First, my material must be "interesting"—that is, in some way different from anyone else's. Second, I must *know* when I'm telling the truth; one doesn't always know. Third, the theory that anyone's story is interesting if truthfully told is not true. The theory that "everyone has at least one story to tell" *is* true, but, unless he has natural genius, or emotions of overpowering intensity, he will write or tell it unconsciously, and it won't be a good story. Unconsciousness produces those débordements of emotion which nauseate a reader. The nausea is caused because the emoting author isn't aware that he is overflowing. This is embarrassing, in life or in art.

Then comes the final test. Even if I succeed in being truthful, and if I relate interesting facts, I may still fail. I must have some knowledge of métier or my writing will have a taint, that curse of curses: domestic writing.

Rules for good writing, I sometimes think, are like rules for good behaviour: be yourself, be simple and easy and honest, be aware of yourself and your audience, and don't exaggerate (dramatize) unless you can do it à propos.

But why talk of rules, since a born writer breaks them all whenever he needs or wants to? Or is it true that there are some he never breaks? I think so; principally that one about overflowing.

Not being a born writer, I try to remember most of the rules —especially that one about refusing to lie. Is it true that the emotions I'm feeling today, and trying to write about, are the same ones I felt years ago and tried to write about? Yes, it is true. Because long before Georgette's death we had all learned something (from Orage) about the seven tests for weighing emotions:

The seven characteristics of emotion
1. What kind of emotion are you having?
2. Its appropriateness (does the emotion fit the occasion?).
3. Its intensity (always a value even if the emotion is so-called mean).
4. Its elevation (the object to which it is applied).
5. Its degree of expression (is it articulate, has it finesse?).
6. Its universality (not common, but affirmed—the authenticity of a human emotion).
7. Its individuality (character of you, unique).

The morning after Georgette's funeral a strange thing happened. I wakened with my head turned slightly down to the left, as if there were a deep well just below the bed and, as I bent down to listen, I heard her voice coming up to me out of the well, telling me all those special things she alone seemed to know. This is exactly what happened, and it happened several times. But I could never remember what she had said.

Then, in the following days, I had a recurrent dream. It went like this:

I had said au revoir to her for a few days, as I sometimes used to do, leaving Paris or the lighthouse or the château with a friend for a trip in the car. In the dream I would try to telephone to her from Rouen or Caudebec or Les Andelys because I'd had a premonition that she had something to tell me. But the telephone wouldn't work, I couldn't reach her, I became anxious; was she waiting for my call, did she think that I hadn't heard her, or that I wouldn't respond? No, she never thought *wrong*. I decided that I must rush back to Paris or Tancarville, because nothing mattered to me so much as to be where she was.

I drove fast, too fast, and I arrived. I saw her again, looked once more at her incomparable face, felt once more her enfolding presence—that total presence which always came toward me as if she were carrying her life in her arms, putting it at my disposal, rescuing me from all the alien forces of the world.

The dream always ended as she greeted me—"Mon trésor du ciel, tu es là!"—smiling her unforgettable smile, holding out her arms to me across the room; and, waking, I would lie very still and wonder (again) if anyone else in the world had ever had such a friend. No, I said, no one; and I would try to find words for my conviction. When such a presence (I thought) is embodied in the extraordinary beauty that was hers, when such beauty is incarnated in the kind of being that she was, and when such being is expressed in the kind of artist that she was . . . oh, I know that others have beauty, and authority of presence, and resources of art, but never, never—I'm sure of it —have these gifts existed, in combination, with a nature so cultivated, a mind so full of grace, as she was given at birth. Every day for twenty years I was conscious of wonder.

I have always liked André Maurois because of something he wrote long ago (I quote from memory): "The death of a person you have loved in this way leaves you ever after with a serene courage."

Having had what I have had, I now have enough courage for three lifetimes. Or rather, I have a feeling that courage is never needed.

———

There was never any use trying to explain Georgette's special knowledge to the unknowing. Whenever I tried to talk about her objectively, there was always someone who longed to help me out, and who killed the conversation by saying, "She was really just *everything* you like, wasn't she?" I said, "I'm not talking personally." "Then try to explain what you mean." "I can't explain it quickly or easily or deeply," I said. "All I know is that she was different from everyone else."

"But isn't everyone different from everyone else?"

"Of course. But what was 'different' in Georgette was 'interesting.' It was a different difference—unlike anyone's."

Then I would try to define the difference:

I have always had a passion for impeccable human behaviour, and Georgette's had daily and unfailingly shown me what it is, what it can be. Compared to common behaviour, hers was as uncommon as that of Dostoievsky's "idiot."

For years I had been judging all human conduct by hers,

and I had never found anyone who has acted infallibly from the same standards of excellence. If you tried to emulate her you could surpass your own standards; and if you couldn't understand, she was always willing to respond with illuminations.

But she hadn't only "willingness of heart." Her heart was childlike, therefore unsentimental, therefore discriminating. No one could be more scathing than she about les bêtises humaines; but her treatment of people who indulged in them always had the quality of mercy. Her heart gave the years of our lives together a glory, as if we were always living "les adorables idées." That is why I can now be alone, and not lonely. Today when I have to face a crisis of grief or despair, I am able to find extra strength, as if someone were fighting beside me. The strength comes from knowing what she would have said and done. I am always remembering that she could have explained it all.

Great behaviour, to me, is like great literature—that extra something that becomes Art.

Every day of my life, I think, I have been stating that there is no happiness comparable to knowing that you are always understood, no matter how blithering your conduct may be. This is the guarantee that Georgette offered, and it is the most rewarding of freedoms. Yet I came to know that it is only a by-product of an even higher freedom—impersonal—that of free movement in the realm of "all things counter, original, spare, strange." But I mustn't limit her to an understanding of the happy few. Anyone, in any realm, could be understood by a heart like hers. She understood people so well that she never let those capable of understanding nothing suspect their failure. This may have been a mistake—it gave her a reputation of being without judgment. She *had* judgment, she valued true judgment, but she distrusted the judgment of people who hadn't the finesse to conceal their judging. On the principle, I suppose, that everything divine goes on light feet.

We had a tombstone made of white marble—a small, simple slab—and on it put a fragment of a poem Georgette had written a month before her death:

> Mon dieu, je ne suis qu'une chose
> Qui repose
> Entre vos mains.

And on the eighth of February, Georgette's birthday, Solita sent us her poem:

"ELEGIE POUR GEORGETTE"
Beneath this obligated mound
The small bones lie all derelict,
The heart's high cone and core extinct,
The emptied universal head,
The drained thalassic eyes.

Each day she searched the sky for signs—
What will this new day bring to me?
What chronicle of joy or pain?
Oh, lovely life, don't pass me by,
Or any mystery.

Step gently here, and gently kneel,
Delicate dust retains her clouds
Of visions, a mirage, and spring
Perpetual of rain and roses—
God and the lamb beside.

June 1942. Eight months after Georgette's death, when Americans who had stayed on in France were threatened with concentration camps, Monique decided that I must leave for America.

. . . From Cannes into Spain, where I had my first cup of coffee in three years; on to Madrid, where I had just time for an hour in the Prado; then to Lisbon, where I went to the best hotel and ordered two sidecars, and afterward strolled through the streets, stopping to gaze at shops filled with food I had forgotten the look of. And one night I saw Thornton Wilder's *Our Town.*

Then I was on the S.S. *Drottingholm,* bound for New York, where I didn't know what threatened . . .

The second day at sea I was sitting on the promenade deck, trying to forget where I was and where I was going, seeing only the grave I was leaving behind. The sun was bright and at the open end of the promenade I saw a tall woman in blue—that summer blue of Cannes, always worn with a touch of red—leave her chair and walk across the deck. Her hair was gold, her eyes were bluer than her dress . . . eyes of a visionary or a mystic, I thought. She held her head high, looking at the horizon, seeing no one.

At dinner I asked my table companions who she was. They were surprised that I didn't know. "Dorothy Caruso," they said. "She's been talking to us in the salon all afternoon, telling stories about Caruso that made us weep."

A femme du monde with visionary eyes? Incongruous, impossible, I thought.

The next day I saw her again. She was sitting at a table with three men. They were talking, she was listening . . . listening with a special quality of attention. In her absorption she stroked her hair back from her forehead, slowly and rhythmically.

The next day she saw me sitting in the salon and introduced herself. "I hear you published the *Little Review,*" she said. "My daughter Jacqueline writes poetry, and I wondered if you'd be kind enough to give her some criticism."

"Of course," I said, "gladly. But perhaps she won't like my verdict. I'm supposed to be such a drastic critic. Is her poetry good?"

"I think so, perhaps. I don't know. But criticism might help her."

The poetry wasn't very good, and I was pleased when my reservations were accepted impersonally.

The next day . . . "What do you consider the important thing in the education of children?"

"I don't know anything about children," I said. "Great poetry, great prose, science . . ."

Twenty-four hours from New York. We sat on the boat deck at midnight. The ship was dark, the sea and sky were dark, the night was silent except for the soft beat of engines and the wash of receding waves. I don't know why—except that her eyes were so questioning and so still—but I began to talk about Gurdjieff. I tried, in a vague abstract way, to give an idea of his theory and his teaching, his conception of the possible evolution of humanity—all that had been the basis of our lives since 1924.

At two o'clock we said good night. I went to my cabin. "I wonder why I talked about Gurdjieff?" I asked myself. "Nothing will come of it, and in the morning all will have been forgotten."

But at eight o'clock the next morning someone knocked at my cabin door. "I just want to know if you'll go on talking to-

day," Dorothy Caruso said. "I must hear more about Gurdjieff."
We became friends.

(Later she told me that, after saying good night, she had
found Gloria and Jackie* waiting for her. "I told them that I
had been hearing things that could change our lives.")

---

* Her daughters, Gloria, and Jacqueline Ingram, daughter of a second
marriage.

New York City, the Fourth of July, 1942.

An unfamiliar place—hard and garish and gigantic after twenty years in the gentle countryside of France. We were overwhelmed.

"What shall we do?" Dorothy said. "I'd better take a skyscraper for your friends and mine and the children's."

Then we realized that neither of us had many friends left in New York. Some had died, some had fallen away because of different ways of life; some had lost all interest for us, or we for them. I had a small group of real friends—those who had been with Gurdjieff during the years in France and who were now in New York. They became Dorothy's friends, too.

And then we found a house—237 East Sixty-first Street. We called it the rose-stone house. There were plane trees in front of it and a garden behind. In the dining-room, which opened on the garden, stood the long fourteenth-century Florentine table at which Dorothy and Caruso used to sit, examining his coin and stamp collections on the nights when he wasn't singing.

We went on talking. We talked about our memories of Enrico and Georgette. There is always vitality in talk about great existences. All lesser talk becomes pallid: like dinner-table talk, which I no longer have to listen to; the social anecdote offered over and over, its raconteurs forgetting how many times they have repeated it; or talk about art objects in apartments overflowing with their accumulation, so that there remains no space for personal existence in rooms overwhelmed with African sculpture; no place where the eyes can rest because they are always confronted with some masterpiece good for an hour's loose and arty dissertation. This wasn't our way. We couldn't spend our time in private museums or public persiflage.

We talked of Italy, of France; not only of their monuments and treasures, but of the impressions made on us by living for years in their landscapes and civilizations.

"Italy is a rigid country," Dorothy said. "Immovable. Nothing moves. It's a background. In the great pictures it's the background that counts—the figures bend, not the landscape. Cypress trees—no shadows, no leaf patterns. Italy is a distant country. It's not three-dimensional, it's a silhouette. You're always looking from a distance. Italy is lovely from train windows."

"You talk like a painter, or a writer," I said. "Haven't you ever written anything?"

"No—just some little poems . . . a long time ago."

"Hasn't anyone ever told you to write?"

"No."

"Haven't you known any writers?"

"Yes . . . Wells, Somerset Maugham, Alexander Woolcott, Janet Flanner, Michael Arlen, Louis Bromfield . . ."

"Didn't they notice your talk?"

"I didn't talk, I listened to them. They were writers—I admired them."

"You talk in images," I said, "the language of the emotions. No one encouraged you to talk after Caruso died. No one needed your thought or your emotions. In self-defense you made yourself into a femme du monde. That wasn't interesting. You don't have to go on being that. You're a born writer."

Her father was a writer. Her grandfather, too, who was also a friend of Poe.

She was the last great friendship of my life, and she died in 1955. She was sixty-two—young, lovely, handsome and strong; and I couldn't believe she would die.

Someone said to me the other day, "I can't even imagine what it would be like to have such friends as you've had."

My two great friends had many qualities in common. Both had the kind of creative imagination that brings ideas to life, and the special talent of thoughtfulness that promises the expansion of an idea as the days pass. Dorothy gave the impression of never speaking without first having thought; Georgette gave the impression of having instantly created. Even in the dispersions of social badinage, Dorothy always managed to say only the reflective thing. In this, Georgette was unlike her: how often she used to say that the unreality of salon talk offered her an irresistible toboggan-slide into almost any irresponsible utterance.

Both had the most remarkable visual memory and the ability to suggest on paper, in a few swift lines, the very essence of a human being—as did Jane and Janet.

"What is his wife like?" someone asked Georgette. "She is a comma," she said. One day, watching Nancy Cunard's beautiful walk, Dorothy said, "She is like a tree walking." And describing a certain man she said, "His eyes stood motionless, as if he were looking at me through his thoughts." Once, on a promenade, two friends of Georgette's—one very tall, one very short—were walking ahead of her: "Un franc cinquante," she said. And once when she was desperately ill at the American Hospital in Paris, there were large oxygen tanks lurking somewhere in the room, like monstrous, misshapen beasts. The doctor was half-lifting her in the bed when she said suddenly, barely able to speak but noticing the tanks, "J'estime beaucoup les éléphants!"

185

Georgette was the born artist whose every word, gesture and act bore the wise—or fatal—artist's signature. Dorothy was a born writer who didn't know it and didn't begin to write (seriously) until she was fifty.

Both had simplicity, by which I mean a kind of essentiality. Both had few "manifestations"—gestures without meaning. Both were unselfconscious, "natural." Neither ever "put on an act" in her daily life, though both could play a flawless public rôle —Dorothy because she had learned she had to, Georgette because she sometimes wanted to. Neither had a trace of that indiscriminating, sentimental, pretentious, portentous, arty nature that is so quiveringly embarrassing. Both had the kindest kind of mockery, but Georgette's self-mockery was the more inclusive. Both, more often than not, put others' needs above their own. Both had an indestructible valour and courage, and both faced death as a rôle to be played in a way that would save those they loved from despair.

Both had the same sinister maladie, the same humiliating operation. Both were condemned long in advance, and neither showed that she knew it, though afterward, in Dorothy's diary, I found these words: "I've been feeling so badly—partly from my back, partly my arm, and mostly my head. Couldn't find the future any more—it was all hidden in a fog—and I began to realize that the past was fading too. Frightening this: to have only the present left, and that limited by aches, and illness, and that question, that awful question . . ."

In the weeks before death both used the same phrase over and over. One said, "C'est trop beau"; the other, "It's too beautiful." Every time I came into a room Dorothy said, "I'm so *glad* to see you." Georgette said, "Mon chef d'oeuvre, merci pour ton existence." Dorothy said, "So many leaves are falling this year," and "Living here like this with you is like living in heaven."

Sometimes now at night, when I'm afraid of being too sad to sleep, I repeat a poem that Georgette wrote to me long ago.

"Remember," I say to myself, "remember that this poem was written to *you*. Is it possible?"

> Vous m'avez emmenée si loin
> Sur les routes du ciel
> Qu'à mon dernier matin
> Mon sourire dira:
> "Ne vous inquiétez pas—
> Je connais le chemin."

> You have led me so far
> Along the roads of heaven
> That on my last morning
> My smile will say:
> "You must not be afraid—
> I know the way."

Solita thinks the translation should be less "bare," like this:

> So far have you led me
> By all of heaven's ways
> That on my final morning
> My smile will say:
> "Have no fear for me—
> I know so well the way."

Which one do I prefer? "By all of heaven's ways" is beautiful, but . . . As to the last line, I like the everyday simplicity of "I know the way." It is a conversation.

———

"I think continually of those who were truly great," said Spender. They are those who impress their image upon you forever and inspire you with a deathless love. And you continue to make discoveries about them that bring revelations you hadn't expected. I once wrote to Solita about one of mine:

As I told you long ago, it was only after Georgette's death that I suddenly thought one day: "She loved me too." I had always

187

been so absorbed in my love for her, in my gratitude for having found her, that I hadn't had time to think of any particular reason why she should love me.

Now I know why. I really know now, because of what has happened to me. I have a broken heart, that's what's the matter, that's all there is to it. The meaning of the old phrase is clear to me now.

But why is my heart broken? And does what has happened justify me in talking of heartbreak? I think so. And this is why:

Whatever state or degree of "being" Georgette and Dorothy possessed, their being was to me a vital life background. Not only because we had a supercommunication, but because their existences were affirmative in relation to mine, never negative, never depressing in that awful atmosphere of the lukewarm. They *went on* with things. They made something of whatever it was that my "being" offered. They *invited* my being, they *encouraged* my life. They had some quality that makes life *go*. And now I understand that I had this for them too. No one else will want it from me now. Monique appreciates it, enjoys it, needs it; but her life would keep going without it. It's enough for her that we are together. I'm talking about something more impersonal— like a childish demand that "something wonderful must happen." So it always did.

And now that no one will ask me to use this (perhaps my only) gift, I look into a void. It is made of the loss of love and the loss of function—a double aloneness for which I have not been prepared or trained, and which can be described, I think, as a broken heart.

This is as clear a formulation as I can make today. Except to add that revelation is more important than pain.

And now that I've finished defining, it occurs to me that I will have further revelations, bringing new understanding. Shall I come to realize that a "broken heart" is merely self-pity? I don't think so. My tears have the feeling of self-pity, but my heartbreak stands aloof and observing, and it has no tears.

There is another kind of heartbreak, and Solita once defined it. She wrote:

I, too, once had a broken heart, and it stayed broken ever after; it never lived again. Some kind of organic growth replaced it, something that has functioned like a heart at times and turned me toward God, nature, impersonal emotions, large and small. Through this event I came to know another world—the world of the broken heart. One of its aspects is that it doesn't need or want anything "wonderful" to happen. Everything has already happened and nothing can ever be "wonderful" any more—just good, better—bad or worse. Sometimes worst.

And there is still another kind. It comes from no thought of, or pity for, one's self, and it brings deeper tears. It is pity for someone else's hidden, silent, valiant, longing, wishful, fear-filled, hurt-filled, humour-filled life—Dorothy's life. I have this heartbreak too now, and it is the kind that never ends.

Oh, I am not complaining—I wouldn't dare. Someone who inspires great love gives you so much to think about that you never come to the end of your remembrances. You have no time for self-pity, and you have no need for courage; you have no space for loneliness, and you are fortified against emptiness. I think of a little poem by von Munchausen, "Words spoken about a grave":

Uber ein Grab hin

Je länger du dort bist
Um so mehr bist du hier;
Je weiter du fort bist
Um so näher bei mir.

Du wirst mir notwendiger
Als das tägliche Brot ist;
Du wirst lebendiger
Je länger du tot bist.

189

Spoken about a Grave

The longer you have been there
The longer you are here.
The farther you are from me
The more I feel you near.

You were my necessity
As is one's daily bread;
And you are all of life to me
The longer you are dead.

Once I was lost, but not lonely; and once I was lonely but not
lost. Now I am not lost, and not lonely—I am loved; that is, I
remember that I *was* loved, and that such an event has a present
and a future as well as a past.

PART TWO

REMEMBRANCE OF THINGS PAST

The day I die

Nineteen-fifty-six. Riderwood, Maryland.* I have been thinking, during this lovely, lonely and breathless spring . . . day after day I have been thinking of the day I die.

The forest in my window, old and strong, will live on after me for a hundred years. Every leaf on every tree will die, but in spring will seem to live again. Days will end and begin again; clouds will form and float forever; rain will renew the earth; snow will slowly form and fall and form again, but I, the rejoicer, will not be here. The chairs and tables in my room are four hundred years old, but they still have a long life before them. My red carpet will not fade so quickly as I shall have faded, and my blue armchair—heaven blue—will still stand in its place. Who else will find, in sorrow or enchantment, the comfort it has offered me? A book on a table, a face on a photograph

---

* After Dorothy's death I lived on in Riderwood, waiting for May and my return to France.

. . . the only evidence that I have existed; a young face with beauty in it. I have kept it there as a defiance to time and fading. Can this have been me?

And this "me" who will have died—will its death matter to anyone? Yes, three people still on earth will say "the difference to me." Four others will miss me for a little while. Seven people out of the planet's billions . . . seven people out of a lifetime of people, friends, loves and experience . . . and I dare to say that such a life has mattered? Yes, because it has mattered so much to me—my breathless life, I say, how can it quiet itself for death?

And before dying, shall I never live again beside a mountain? In France, above Cannes . . . there is my village with its mountain range along the sea. At twilight the sun sinks between low curving ridges and the mountain outlines become blue and mauve shadows; an hour later the lights of Cannes bloom in the night, the sea has no movement and the countryside slips into a peace so long and silent that it suggests eternity. I don't want to die until I have lived for a year in this silence of evening, as if in preparation for the silence of death.

How I long not to die—to continue in an endlessness of days I have already lived. What is it that so allures me? What is it that I do when I do nothing? I wait, I expect to be exalted. I take a walk, I stand in a window, I look at a view. I should by now be "growing old," but I don't believe it; I am still looking and feeling and thinking with an endless energy that is like an exercise in delight.

The events of the world have held little of my engrossed attention, and my events have been little noticed by the world. No real event, for me, has ever had more than four people in it; my greatest events have had only three, or two; some of my most enduring ones have had only myself as spectator. And how strange it is that, in memory, the single ones—fleeting but permanent—flash first across my mind, as if the others were too treasured to appear at once. How many times do I remember the event of saying over and over, through different years, "Trim the dim tapers, for I see no dawn"—a poem whose title I have forgotten, whose author perhaps I never knew. Why do I remember so often a single high meadow grass, tipped against a crescent moon, the sea on one side and a mountain beyond? Or how often have I repeated, in moments of doubt and faith, a great formulation that made the world almost intelligible: "Form is an expression of force and is moulded into the purpose of the impulse that engendered it." When I first heard it, I thought quickly of a tree. Why do I remember a day in New York when I saw a Noel Coward film, *The Astonished Heart,* and rode in a taxi afterward, repeating in awe, mile after mile, "And He shall smite thee with madness and blindness and astonishment of heart." Or why am I suddenly in France again, at a table in a little garden, drinking a glass of rose-coloured wine?

My heart has always been astonished. Therefore I am too young to die. I was born to be forty; I should have liked to be forty years young for a thousand years. It will be unnatural to die, to feel no more "How beautiful this day has been, this poem, this music!" . . . Until the day I die I shall continue to live in a world where people were vibrant and expectant, where they had clear and thoughtful hearts, where they made poems that can never be forgotten:

> . . . From my hour of birth.
> Upon my buried body lie
> Lightly, gentle earth.

. . . not in a world where no one notices these *b*s and *l*s which might transport him to a realm above the one in which he lives —the unreal, created, and imposing realm called Art.

"QUE LE JOUR RECOMMENCE . . ."

THE MAGIC OF FRANCE

May, 1956. I have come back to France to live forever, and I am now at the beginning of the end of my life. On my little garden table there are five radishes and a glass of white wine.

I am writing in the Chalet Rose, in Le Cannet. The winding streets of this village lead down to the dazzling seafront shops of Cannes, the playground where Americans love to spend their summers.

In our little house two miles above Cannes (our wartime house, where Georgette died), Monique and I live far from cities, people, and events. I no longer feel the incessant need of "doing something." In Le Cannet I have nothing to do except what I now call doing: reading and thinking and writing, walking and looking, talking and sleeping, laughing and dreaming, listening to music and rain, celebrating sunlight and moonlight, and giving thanks for all these things.

I've always heard people say, "When I am older I shall do all the things I've never had time to do before." And then they never find time to do any of them. It is because of bereavement that I now have time, and I doubt that one ever finds such time until one is bereft. It is then that the turning seasons become almost the prime reasons for living.

I realize that few people are fortunate enough to become recluses, that very few would want to, and that many would disapprove of my present sane and sheltered world. But how *should* one live in one's sixties and seventies? Surely not as one has always lived before. Statesmen, diplomats, scientists, lawyers, journalists, politicians, businessmen, soldiers, heroes, presidents, and kings are forced to live in fixed moulds. I am outside these species. I am living in a new cycle—one which leaves me, at the end of things, with a new beginning.

I found the Chalet Rose in desperation, and inspiration, during the war. Peering through a small window I saw a room with a view—olive trees and the sea. I sought out the proprietor. Would he rent his private pavillon? He had never thought of doing it, but he would. For how much, monsieur? For 400 francs a month, mademoiselle.

A box of a house, hung among pine, palm and olive trees, surrounded by wild hyacinths, roses and camellias. Its windows look out over the Mediterranean, the Carlton Hotel in Cannes, and the ancient church and clocktower of Suquet; they look up at vineyards and mountains and a long shaded canal. Its front door is on the Avenue Victoria at the western end. The Aga Khan's villa, Yakimour, is at the other end.

Beside our front door there is a little slit of a letterbox, and letters from all over the world drop to the floor of our miniscule salon, still furnished with bits and pieces as it was during the war.

. . . Three rooms, no bath. Is this a privation, after the luxury of other days? No. If you ask me how much I love France I will answer, "Enough to live without a bathroom." No greater love . . . And then I have only to remember wartime. We were in this house, we had almost no money, almost no food, almost no heat, almost no light. Anything we did have took on an immense value. And so it does now. As I look back, it is marvelous to live more in imagination than in abundance.

People who have never lived through a war can never imagine its civilian torments. Day after day you feel you won't be able to endure another moment of hunger. I remember one day when we had only a little pile of pois chiches (chick peas) for our two meals, and I remember walking around the kitchen table looking at them, trying to resist the temptation (and resisting it) to eat just one more before lunch. We had no butter or fats; we had a kind of ersatz sugar, and coffee that bore no relation to any drink we had known; we had one bottle of wine a week (for three people), and it was a gala day when we could buy a few carrots and make a salad of their tops. Sometimes we had a little meat—many people ate horse meat, when they could get it. We had no milk. Sometimes a confectioner's shop produced curious, half-sweetened little pastries. We could usually buy rutabagas, which made people and animals swell up. And no one had soap that would lather, so we sometimes had to use a pair of sheets for a month—or longer. Once I had to steal candles from a church to give us a little light.

Just as I have never forgotten my hatred of school, and never wake now on Monday mornings without rejoicing in my freedom from it, so I have never forgotten the taste of war hunger. And today, sitting in our triangular garden (six feet long at the triangle's base—just enough space for a table, three green chairs and three pots of pink geraniums), I salute every easily found (expensive) item of food as if it were manna. And

199

who could complain, after living through a war, of baths from a tea-kettle? Not I. Nor do I hate drinking-water that is tepid—I who, in America, can't live without ice water or my nightly cocktail. Here I never think of a cocktail. In Paris I do, because there I see people who are still engaged in "activities," and in such a situation you must ease tensions with cocktails.

Instead of activities, I indulge in what I consider actions: the active planning of hours and days to be spent in privacy, profit, pleasure, purpose and peace. Instead of the six-o'clock cocktail hour, I make a ceremony of five o'clock, to watch the beginning of twilight and devote myself to my nostalgias.

————

Mid-August, and the moment when stars fall. So far I have seen only one.

The light of August . . . that month when silence can be heard behind the singing of insects; half-summer, half-autumn; sun, mist, shadows; the Midi of France where the sun shines for a hundred days at a time, where trees and flowers and shrubs intoxicate the senses, where grilled gates disclose half-hidden gardens, where peasants bend over their vines and move slowly along the lanes, where pine-cone fires burn through the evenings.

In this ambiance our lovely French days move in their lovely way. I contrast them with my last days in America . . .

In Riderwood, snow fell all day in our forest, flaking our windows, enclosing us in a German fairytale. We had swift heat by a turn of a thermostat; instant coffee before the television (NBC morning news), and a daily rebellion against colloquial American speech as we braced ourselves to hear "like" used with a verb. Then we shopped in a supermarket, where no tomato with a flavour can be found. Then lunch, on a lace-draped table set against wine-red Renaissance velvet. Then a hope, at last, of time to think and write; but no, we must take out the car and drive before the light fades, and come back to a warm house and the temptation to advance the cocktail hour. Then news on TV and dinner eaten on trays in order not to miss a new drama that might contain some psychological excitement—awful, irresistible urge for anyone under the compulsion to know how stories end, as I am. Then the hope, again, of time to think and write, but no—I continue to vibrate with the obligations of the day and can do nothing but read and sleep. A pleasant but frustrated day. No magic, except that of snow and friendship . . . which of course is enough.

But in France all my day will have magic—not of snow but of sun; of French coffee, black and strong, and croissants at dawn, and four hours of concentrated thought and work—no interruptions except time taken to smell the sea mist and to watch the day rise, which is the opposite of interruption; no turmoil, no voices, no errands, no digressions, no frustrations. Our cook, Elisabeth, comes up from the village, carrying a basket of fragrant tomatoes and fresh green beans, asparagus, veal for a blanquette, estragon, cheese, fruits and wine from the little sidewalk shops.

Elisabeth not only markets and cooks; she scrubs, cleans, dusts, polishes, launders, irons, sews, mends, gardens, does carpentry, makes fires, and so on. For all these services she asks $34 a month.* She spends five hours a day on these chores and goes home at two o'clock. She never steps out of her place and would be horrified if we stepped out of ours. Ours is simply to be served, and protected. She lives by the emotions, but not negative ones— she never does what is known as faire la tête. She is always enthusiastic, she never fails to state that she has la chair de poule if you tell her that your book is going well. And she has

---

* Today, alas, twice that.

the French mania for beauty. I have listened to her gasping over a good-looking American guest: "Ah, mademoiselle, quelle beauté, quel chic, quelle distinction, quelle race!—elle a tout pour elle!"

We have neighbours—French—on both sides of the Chalet Rose, but we are almost unaware of them except when we want to be aware. It would be inconceivable for them to "run in" on us, as American neighbours do. When they want to see us, a servant slips a note into our postbox: "Would it be convenient if I came in for a moment at five o'clock today—or perhaps tomorrow? Bien sympathiquement." When they want to give us flowers they send them by a femme de chambre, "pour ne pas vous déranger."

I work from dawn until noon; then an apéritif in the garden, under the olive trees, as I read over my morning's pages; then lunch, an hour's siesta, a long walk through the hills, and more work as the day descends; supper in a little kitchen—soupe de cresson, a pâté, black olives, radishes, goat's cheese, a light wine; then a book, then a walk under the stars.

I have never had such experience of the night sky. It is like being a shepherd, or like standing on the top deck of a ship, while the universe reels around you.

My life is a mystery, even to myself.

Is it possible that I'm a happy person, living what might be called a prisoner's life within four walls, walking for exercise along an avenue where Monique has walked for twenty years, where I may do the same? Yes, I am happy.

What do I do that so enchants me? I walk beside a canal, overhung with low trees and wild roses, and listen to the rippling water; I sit on a little bridge and smoke a cigarette in the sun; I walk on as in a dream, I smell the air as if it were flowers; at a bend in the road I stop beside the old stone fountain and listen to its endless splashing; bells of the ancient tower clock ring out in the valley . . . how I love the chimed hours—another hour of life gone by, another soon to sound . . . how many more days of hours, months or years of hours, will I have? I descend a long avenue and choose which pine branches I will steal to decorate the Chalet Rose; I walk past the Aga Khan's villa, stop to watch the gardeners planting their flowers, laying out their vegetable beds in strict designs; I pass Pierre Bonnard's pale pink chalet, the most sympathetic small house on this coast; I examine every villa along the avenue—the small ones, not the great angry ones—and peer into their half-abandoned gardens; I choose which ones would be pleasant to live in, and decide how I will change them; I walk down the hill to the Terminus Café, sit on the terrace and drink beer, talk to the taxi man about the price of gas, regard the passing peasants and the new American cars; I watch two Italian workmen mending a hole in the street, and a hotel garçon setting the sidewalk tables for dinner. Then I walk back to the Chalet Rose and watch the men carrying in our wood for winter—small logs of soft pine and hard oak, pine cones and petit bois to start the fires with. After they leave I spend an hour piling the logs in orderly stacks. Then I grind coffee for tomorrow's breakfast. None of these things would I be doing in America.

And then what? I drink a cinzano with Monique in the garden, eat an omelet or a chicken wing, a salade d'endive, cheese, wine. We sit in silence as night comes on. Then what? I read, without interruption—no telephone, no television, no neighbours. I take another walk. I contemplate and speculate. Why am I "happy?" What are my inner springs that keep rewinding themselves? Why am I so immensely contented living as I do in serenity, seclusion, solitude? Is it because I have arrived, appropriately, at putting away childish things? Why do I feel like a source of life? Is it because I am like Georgette, in her poem beginning

> I dreamed that my soul was a welling spring,
> a fountain rising endlessly . . .

The day passes quickly, with all these musings. The sea becomes indigo, and below my window a black and white ship, the *Cristoforo Colombo*, lies in the blue harbour to the left of the old clock tower. I love to sit here looking down at the lights of Cannes. The olive trees are still. Soon the ship will blaze with lights, its siren will sound three long blasts, then a short one, and it will sail away to the south, on its way to Gibraltar and America.

The cicades and cigales sing more loudly, and I remember, as I do every night, what my Nantie told me long, long ago—that all the little creatures in the trees are saying good night to each other.

Sometimes at midnight, when I've been too sad to sleep, I go down to the kitchen and make a pot of strong French coffee and bring it up to my "salon." I sit in a circle of lamplight, drinking and smoking. Outside, over the Mediterranean, it is moonlight. It seems to me that it is always moonlight in Cannes, as it was in San Francisco years ago.

Strong coffee always makes me fall asleep within a half hour. I sleep until four o'clock and then watch another dawn over mountains and sea. Four o'clock in the morning is my time for "thinking," the time when I like to make these notes. Events seem to have happened to me in the night. Something from some unknown somewhere has become known to me.

The egoist and I

"What an egocentric life!" someone says. And I answer, "Why? Once I lived for three years a life that was what others liked. Now I am free to live as *I* like." I am doubly free, because freedom is all I have left. I must make it do. And it does. It fills my void.

"But if others were like you?"

"Most others aren't," I say.

Everyone I know tells me that I mustn't bring "my vital and exciting life" to an end. I am not, I'm giving it a new beginning. That is all I need to say today to justify my withdrawal.

Monique would never ask anyone to justify anything. I suppose she has lived for ninety years without once commenting on a friend's behaviour. I draw from Georgette's description of her as "a fairy-tale nurse, a character met only in books with coloured illustrations, a being whose words and steps make no sound, and who always offers to agree with me." Perhaps she always agrees with me too—I don't know. She may always or sometimes or never; the point is that she makes it unnecessary to know. Her uniqueness to me is not only that she understands me but that she never misunderstands me. I can talk as wildly as I like; she knows that it isn't wild. This leaves me free of the burden of explaining myself; I can function without the superfluity of conflicts, great or small. Therefore I am no longer the aggressive person that people have so often accused me of being. I follow my own impulses, my own rhythms. I do what I most want to do when I most want to do it. I am unhindered.

All this means that I am an egoist. Of course. But what is an unobjectional egoist? Auden defines the difference between an egoist and a selfish man: "A selfish man is one who seeks to satisfy his own desires at whatever cost to others. An egoist is a man whose primary interest is not in objects and things outside himself, but in his own thoughts and feelings."

I am probably as selfish as everyone else—or more so? I don't know. I do know that I have always been overwhelmingly interested in my own thoughts and feelings, often to the exclusion of everything else in the world. To be deprived of time to think and feel them, as I (unselfishly) was in certain years of stress, has always been an agony to me. I understand a poet like Leopardi who said that he could see no landscape but that of his own mind.

Yes, I have been an egoist. My shortcoming is that I've never become a *great* egoist. A great egoist is a person who refuses to be eaten alive; and who also arranges not to eat others. I have often yielded to being eaten rather than to eat others, but I don't believe in such submission. I disapprove of cannibalism in all its forms.

"Satisfying one's desires at whatever cost to others?" With Monique and me there is no cost to either of us, there is only mutual freedom. Living with such a person combines the perfection of living alone with the perfection of perfect comradeship whenever both long for it, or whenever when one does and the other gladly adjusts. Monique is *there*, and that satisfies us both. I am the contributor, she is the receiver—this is the way she wants it to be. I accept such an arrangement with immense gratitude. Neither of us is a vampire.

Monique falls and breaks her arm. The next morning, lying in her horrid cast, she doesn't speak of herself but asks, "Comment vas-tu? As-tu bien dormi?" Such abnegation constantly astonishes me, but I accept it calmly, as agreed, and tell her that I don't know whether I've slept at all, "Je suis trop exaltée avec mon livre, je pense qu'il marche bien." "A la bonheur!" she cries, and I know she won't think about her arm if I can tell her that I've found a good adjective.

She wants to hear what I've written. "I think you've been a little hard in that passage," she says. "Bon," I say, "I'll try to soften it." "And there's one place where your readers will feel you're light-minded." "Really?" I say, "I thought I was being the opposite." "You were," she says, "but they wouldn't know." "I'll try to fix it," I say with pleasure. And our day moves on, in its métier of harmony.

When twilight falls over this brilliant coast, and I wonder, as I so often do, why my life has come to a dénouement less unbearable than the one I prepared myself for, I sit in my window facing the sea and review my day. Has it really been so egocentric? Hasn't it given something to Monique, something in my letters to friends, something to my neighbour, something to my proprietress, something to the hospital (my magazines), and the little orphan boy, and the little old lady in her wheelchair, and the little cat who shares our days? Of course I find that it has given the most to me; and as I gaze at the beauty in my window I plan to reverse this order of things tomorrow. But each tomorrow always leaves the balance in my favour.

THE MYSTERIOUS ENERGY

Two Christmas Eves

Before Christmas Monique fell and broke her hip. There was an operation, but at ninety-two . . . I spent my days at the clinique, and at night drove back to the Chalet Rose.

It was the night before Christmas and all through the house . . . darkness and emptiness and silence. After the long day I was hopeless and helpless, and the night was so black that I didn't see the package waiting on the doorstep. It was a disque from New York—a small disque, and I wasn't prepared for the title that stared at me: "Le Steppe," by Gretchaninoff sung by Mary Garden . . . One of Georgette's great songs, sent by our favourite pianist, Allen Tanner.

I had never heard Mary Garden sing this lonely lament, and to hear her now on Christmas Eve, in a country far, far away from my art-haunted youth—would it be unbearable, or restorative, or both?

I held the record in my hands a long time. I didn't want to play it suddenly, I wanted time to think about it, to realize that it was there; then I would choose the perfect moment to hear it. ("To hear," I remembered, "is passive; to listen is active.") I would know how to listen.

At last I knew exactly what to do. First I would sleep, in anticipation; then I would play the song when it should be played—in the darkness before dawn, as in the opening words: "Sad lies the steppe in its solitude, Nowhere a star in the sky . . ."

I fell asleep on a memory. How many years ago was it, in Étretat, Normandie, that I had played a record on my balcony by the sea, and listened to this unforgettable voice singing "Annie Laurie" and "Sweet Afton"? And the next day had heard Chamberlain announce, "England is now at war with Germany."

Christmas Day. I wakened at five, went down to the kitchen and made coffee, toasted a croissant, and brought the tray upstairs. The disque lay on a small table beside my armchair, and the chair faced the window where the first light would appear. It was still as dark as night, and still I waited. Then, just before the night began to fade, I put the record on my electrophone, set the speed at 78, made my heart stand still, and listened . . .

That night I wrote to Solita:

Oh, the perfection of slightly imperfect things—a Venus without arms, a broken column against the sky . . . Mary Garden, with a voice that won't always do what she wants it to do, but with a conception, a diction, a timbre (in fact, a voice!): the way she pronounces "solitude"; "night comes on shadowy wings"; "never a nightingale sings" (all these consonants so wonderfully softened); "never a star in the sky"—imagine anyone being able to put *sweetness* into a word like "sky." Her opening measures were more tender than Georgette's, which were a little "darker," and I prefer Mary here; but Georgette did the climax on "Oh, ma bien-aimée" without taking a second breath, and people wanted to rise from their chairs as she sang this word. Mary's "my belovèd one" is heartbreaking; and then she ends on that unbelievable consonant softness and sweetness.

I rushed to the clinique—it was still so dark that I had to turn on my headlights, but this French hospital was open all night and you could run in and out as you pleased, there was no one en garde in the entrée. I rushed to Monique's room and told her about the disque, and our life came flooding back to us. Her face!—and her happiness that she would soon be home and could hear the song . . . as least so she pretended. I pretended too, which was all that was necessary. What importance a broken hip, and a back made of cement which nothing can ever soften? Our non-life of the last month vanished and we were new people. Such (may I feebly say) being the influence of great art, the most mysterious of energies.

Solita answered:

Oh, your story of the Garden record! No one but you—and (or with) Monique—in the world today would have had such a flight into lost-forever realms. I saw you rushing to the clinique with your precious adventure, to transport Monique back into the life she loved with Georgette; and remembered her words to you before her operation: "Ma vie a été très belle, I prefer not to wake up from the ether."

Your letter—so a part of our lost world—opened to me the places I have wished (wrongly?) to keep closed, because one can't *work* if one lives longing for the emotional beauties to appear. Why can't there be a balance? To live outside that world is a deprivation not to be borne—to exist for years without sun and air would be a just comparison. In this case "one" is me—only me. How ungrateful I am. I had everything, all the miracles . . . I don't know how to "let go" . . . Must stop thinking in these "young ways," I'm told. Yet they are ageless?

Are they not? Lost-forever realms? Surely Monique and I aren't the only people, even in today's peculiar world, who would respond to this art-moment as we did.

Wishing to pass on our rejoicing to others, I wrote to another friend in Paris about the Garden disque. Her response depressed me:

It has been announced that parts of the lost arms of the Venus have been found on the seabed off the island of Milos . . . but, speaking of "imperfections" and the "imperfect," Mr. Gurdjieff has said many things on a grander scale than you have been conscious of. He spoke of logamanisms in which initiates *consciously* introduced an error. What you are talking about is quite another matter. A broken column against the sky still has perfection because it was *made* perfect in the first place. If something is perfect, every inch of it is—even if only an inch remains through Time. Your example of Mary Garden reveals that there was something imperfect, and nevertheless she did something with it that made it moving or beautiful but not *perfect*. That's why I think it should not have been compared to as perfect a thing as the column. You mix scales. As for the Venus, who, to greater minds and understanding than mine, is not that perfect (she always reminded me especially of something animal—however that's personal) . . . it has never been proved that she didn't have arms in the first place.

I answered this curious (and, I thought, very confused letter) by saying that I wasn't interested in learning anything about the Venus' arms, I was only remembering how we had loved her when we were young; that a broken column is more moving than an intact one for some reason having nothing to do with its initial perfection, and so on. And I ended on an affectionate note, "Dear V., you're crazy."

This brought another letter: "I think I once wrote you that you are one of the nicest people to disagree with. Indeed challenge is good but name-calling is not exactly a noble form of challenge. I'm sorry you found it necessary to do so."

Astounded by this rebuke, Monique and I could only decide that it was my "You're crazy" which had produced it. So I explained that the term was really an endearment, one I invariably used when hoping to start an interesting discussion. Her next reply confounded me: "This time I believe you were what fencing people call touchée, and your return thrust came from a bad place."

I had had enough. I answered: "I'm not merely touchée. Consider me killed. And the 'bad place' you discover in me is just bad enough to have expected a 'So sorry to have misunderstood you.' Evidently you mean to continue to misunderstand, so I can only say that we mustn't meet at Easter as planned. I wouldn't be able to control my explosion."

Thus endeth the art lesson about Venus and arms and columns and art, and I never heard from my friend again.

───────────

Another Christmas Eve

I was four (five?) years old. There was a church and a tree, music and candles, and I heard "Silent Night" for the first time and wanted to cry.

Afterward we walked home in the starry silent night—Grandma, Nantie and I. Nantie said she would walk ahead and light the lamps. Grandma took my hand. Years later people always told me, "Your grandmother was a tower of strength, she was stronger than anyone." Whenever she took my hand I felt her strong energy and life, but she was gentle too, and I knew she would protect me from all harm.

When we reached our house there were two lighted candles on the porch, and I saw something hanging from the doorknocker—a little silver basket . . . Santa Claus had come while we were away. The basket was covered with tinsel and bright balls, and in it, wrapped in my doll's blanket, lay a sleeping kitten—infinitesimal and white, with a large pink bow over one ear.

I have always remembered that this was the night I was born.

ISOLATION

Nineteen-sixty-one. June came, and Monique's death.

I was happy that on the day before she died the radio played "Tristan"—the Prelude and the Liebestod. As the final chords faded I waited to see if she would make her usual comment, not knowing whether she had the strength. She had . . . "C'est surhumain!" she cried, with the same energy she must have expended sixty years ago. Whenever she was asked, "What is your favorite music in the world, if allowed only one choice?" she always cried "Tristan!" as if she were shouting the word in defiance of someone. And on this June day I knew that, even as she faced death, she was angrily remembering Clara Schumann's reaction when she first heard the divine opera—her boredom being so intense that she wanted to leave before the end.

The next day, when I realized that Monique was living her last moments and that she knew it too, all I could think of was, "How lonely she must feel." And all she could say at the end was a whispered concern for our little cat, as she compressed the emotions of ninety-two years of life into three words—"N'abandonnes pas Bébé."

That evening I sat in her room—the same room where Georgette died—and looked at the same view: in the window to the left an olive tree, white-gold; to the right, a tilleul; and above the olive leaves the white scale of a moon in a hazy blue sky. What a still sadness there was in the air and the trees. As if autumn had come.

Debate: "You mustn't go on living alone now, isolated and far from us. You must come to Paris, we should all be together as we grow older."

"Let's not talk about age," I said. "I know nothing about it. I shall like to live alone. *You* live with people all around you, you merge your lives with theirs. I can no longer do that. I live differently now."

"But you mustn't live alone, you'll become a melancholy shadow and talk to yourself."

"I won't become a shadow, I shall become a source. People will want to come and talk with me. And I shall certainly talk to myself. With great pleasure. Why not? Besides, doesn't everyone spend his life talking with himself? Better to talk to yourself than to non-listeners. We used to know what conversation is. Today conversation consists of exclamations interrupted by other exclamations. Do you know anyone now who has listening eyes? No. While you talk, the other person is planning what he will say next."

"You'll become neurasthenic . . ."

"Let's not bring in the psychiatrists. I'm probably as neurasthenic as everyone else. Only I *know* when I am. That's not being a neurasthenic."

It is not *neurasthenia* that makes one prefer one's own way of life.

It is not *egoism* that makes one reject "communication which is limited to external points common to us all and of no interest." (Proust).

It is not *isolation* that makes old days appear better than present ones.

It is not *reminiscence* that "disarrays the wits."

It is not *nostalgia* that causes self-pity. Nostalgia is a challenge and a standard-bearer: an effort to make all one's days resemble one's highest moments.

DEATH AND DREAM

I am not lonely, and I have many good dreams. They occur at moments when I need those "lonely depths of feelings" without which life has no fulness. Even though sad, they linger through the day as if their purpose was to give strength.

. . . This morning I wakened saying, "Oh, my dream . . . the saddest dream one could have."

It was about a boy, very young, who loved his mother so much that he could never tell her, he could only try to stay near her. She was a schoolteacher and he was in her class. He made himself fail time after time so that he could stay in that class. He could watch her as she stood before the blackboard, giving out the lessons; even when she turned her back to the pupils, to write on the blackboard, he could watch her back; it was an assurance that she would never leave him. But he knew the day would come when they would be separated, and he knew he could never bear it.

I realized that I was crying and I got out of bed to write down the dream, for Solita, before it faded. It was a story I could see printed on paper, as if written for the *New Yorker* when they publish one of their expert storytellers.

Solita: "What a dream! You must keep always a record of it. What a lovely story it would make. Can you not try?"

No, I can only express it in those simple words I wrote down, as if they had been dictated to me. To *write* it would require the power of that "strange necessity" without which all that is necessary would be strangely absent . . . as if I neither recognized nor desired the instrumentality of that power, that energy.

216

But I can write about the loss of that energy. It happens often and leaves me baffled. Where does it go when it leaves me? Which is like asking, "Where will my life go when it leaves me?" I'm not being fancy, I'm talking about an impression I've sometimes had, a conviction that there existed in my brain a force, an organ, which has suddenly disappeared. To be without this organ is like another sensation I've had when reading a novel: I take snapshots of the characters' backgrounds which exist in my brain as definitely as if they were factual—for instance, when I read Colette's *Chéri* I *see* his mother's house in Neuilly, standing at right angles to the street—a large white house with beautiful French windows and borders of exquisite French flowers on both sides of the drive as you enter and leave your car in the garden. The house exists so clearly in my brain (mind?) that I could photograph it; but what happens to the photograph when I stop looking at it? Does it no longer exist? If *everything* that exists is *material* (as Gurdjieff taught), of what substance is this imagined house composed? Could I touch it? Could I photograph it? If I were a painter I could paint it; as I'm not, I can only live in it—enter by the front door, pass from room to room. What a salon! What a dining room! I see the table where the characters are dining when Chéri says to his mother, "I gather that your memory is breaking down. Do you think anything short of solitary confinement will cure it?"*

In a world to come, in which we may communicate by telepathy instead of words, will we be able to sHow these mental photographs by a sort of cerebral wireless?

Enough madness . . . It's now morning and I return to what is left, still left, of my photogenic life. It consists of one indestructible element: the fact that I am still living, and allowed to live, now as then.

---

* Janet Flanner's translation.

"ET QUE LE JOUR FINISSE . . ."

IF ONLY IN THE HEART'S EMBRACE

Nineteen-sixty-one. Night after night, before sleeping, I sit again on my bench on the Avenue Victoria. Above the dip in the mountains a shining, white-gold, crescent moon rises. To the left, toward Nice, the sea and sky merge; to the right, the mauve Esterels lie in the dying light, and in the space between me and the mountains and the lovely crescent rise the tips of meadow grasses. The smell of a French September fills the warm air. The stillness is total, except for the flight of a swallow or the distant bark of a lonely dog. One by one, night after night, lights bloom over Cannes and the roof-tops and the trees.

. . . My lovely companions are not faded and gone. All I have to do is to remember. Sometimes memory becomes so insistent that I say, "I shall take a walk with my imagination."

One of my ghost companions walks with me as the sun sinks behind the mountains—a sun with no shining light. I am confused and think it is a large pink moon.

"It's all too lovely," the faint far voice is saying. "I do see why you want to stay on here."

We walk again as the moon rises, high above the sea. And the phantom voice quotes words I have always remembered—words that Jane wrote years ago in her experience of early sorrow I had not yet known: "Those zones of pain where one may rest, and of old joys where one may suffer." "Ah yes," says the voice dimly beside me, "I see you rightly staying on . . . you are so close to moonlight here."

Sometimes it is the little ghost of Monique who is waiting for me when I come back from my walk. As the perfect companion, she never fails to say "Racontes!," as if the quiet Avenue Victoria has been full of adventure for me, as indeed it has. I say, "I have had an experience," and tell her of the bright gardens I saw against the changing colours of the sea. "Raconte" is a verb I love, and I have much to tell.

But Monique is one of those listeners who seldom talks, and sometimes I need to listen. This too I can do. I have only to reread a letter Dorothy wrote to me a year before she died, after reading a passage from this book:

> In "The Day I Die" you have written words that make the heart ache. You have produced a sense of suffering within a sense of happiness, and within the suffering a sense of sadness, and within that a feeling of finding a single sorrow; and in the center of all these circles *you* seem to stand—clear-sighted, certain, strong. This curved combination is therefore inevitable; and your acceptance of it, and your gratitude for having been given a few years of it, is expressed in words of true evocation. It isn't exactly the way you talk—it is the way you *are*, as I know you.

Was it so very long ago that Georgette died, in this room where I am sitting? Is 1941 a long, long time ago? Her voice reaches me clearly, across years that have flowed by like living water . . .

What does she say, here, tonight, as in other years? Always she speaks of Gurdjieff, always in the same words that eased my heart and encouraged my effort: "You will go on, you will not forget all that we learned from him, all that we saw him accomplish. Do you remember the day we watched him walking slowly in a crowd near the Galeries Lafayette, moving like a being apart from other men, bearing in his presence the weight of his function and obligation and unfelt by the crowd which, unknowing, left a little space around him?"

UNDER THE WIDE AND STARRY SKY

It was on my Avenue Victoria bench, during the war and Georgette's fatal illness, that I lived in a world where Nature was more important to me than it has ever been since—a world that was made of sky and stars. Every night I sat on the bench and looked at Orion, and I had never known that life could be so full of meaning, so rich and deep that it held us up, our entente so strong that it could even stop pain. Now, years later, I enter that remembered world again. Last night, sitting once more on my bench, memory began to pull me back into our monde à côté: a moment of paralysis, then a sensation of floating; and then, as definitely as one can walk out of one house into another house, I stepped out of the world I live in today and walked into that other world which was our home. It was a full world, and to live outside it can be like living without food and light and air.

———————

I wonder why I have wanted to write this story of my life. I know it at first hand, but so incompletely that it has little meaning. It has been so happy and so sad, as happy as flowers, as sad as moonlight—a happy life that loves the saddest music. It has been a striving and a failing; a development and a diminution; it has been proud, and egotistic, and modest; aggressive and unassuming; alert and unconscious; hopeful and, I fear, lost. It has overflowed with thankfulness and remorse—a life like any other, but which has seemed to me so different, so special, and so blessed as to be unique. The blessings I wanted were love and music, books and great ideas and beauty of environment. I have had them all, and to a degree beyond my asking, even beyond my imagining.

To France

Now winter has come again. There is no snow, but all is winter white, and thin white lines of smoke rise from the chimneys and drift across the pale sky.

How I love this country where I have found such a deep and active peace. Spaceships surround the earth, but I sit in a room where I am surrounded by tuberoses; their white and perfumed life vibrates in the air. I have a fire, I have a cup of coffee, I am conscious of living a minute at a time—minute after minute of lighting a cigarette, of holding out my hands to the fire. Minute by minute, by these small acts, I push aside for an hour those recurrent thoughts of destruction and death that are now much with me.

If I have more years to live, I hope they will be lived in this place. And so I say:

To France, with love. With gratitude for all that has happened to me here; for all that I may still be allowed to feel, to think, to remember and to celebrate in what remains for me of a life on earth.

Le Cannet, Alpes Maritimes, France